RUDOLF STEINER (1861–1925) called his spiritual philosophy 'anthroposophy', meaning 'wisdom of the human being'. As a highly developed seer, he based his work on direct knowledge and perception of spiritual dimensions. He initiated a modern and universal 'science of spirit', accessible to anyone willing to exercise clear and unprejudiced thinking.

From his spiritual investigations Steiner provided suggestions for the renewal of many activities, including education (both general and special), agriculture, medicine, economics, architecture, science, philosophy, religion and the arts. Today there are thousands of schools, clinics, farms and other organizations involved in practical work based on his principles. His many published works feature his research into the spiritual nature of the human being, the evolution of the world and humanity, and methods of personal development. Steiner wrote some 30 books and delivered over 6000 lectures across Europe. In 1924 he founded the General Anthroposophical Society, which today has branches throughout the world.

FROM JESUS TO CHRIST

*Eleven lectures given in Karlsruhe between
4 and 14 October, 1911*

RUDOLF STEINER

RUDOLF STEINER PRESS

Translated by Charles Davy

Rudolf Steiner Press
Hillside House, The Square
Forest Row, RH18 5ES

www.rudolfsteinerpress.com

Published by Rudolf Steiner Press 2005

First published in English in 1930. This reprint is a facsimile of the revised
edition of 1991

Originally published in German under the title *Von Jesus zu Christus*
(volume 131 in the *Rudolf Steiner Gesamtausgabe* or Collected Works) by
Rudolf Steiner Verlag, Dornach. This translation is published by permission of
the Rudolf Steiner Nachlassverwaltung, Dornach

Translation © Rudolf Steiner Press 1991

A catalogue record for this book is available from the British Library

ISBN 1 85584 195 9

Cover by Andrew Morgan Design
Printed and bound in Great Britain by 4edge Limited

CONTENTS

SYNOPSIS OF CONTENTS

This synopsis is in no way authoritative, but is only for the possible convenience of students.

away entirely? Answer given by human consciousness at three different epochs of history — Greek, Buddhist, Ancient Hebrew.

Redemption of the physical body foreseen by Job.

Examples of simplest expression of highest truths in writings of John the Apostle and Paul. The Resurrection; modern scientific opinion. Passages from Paul and John examined. Paul and the Event of Damascus. 'The Risen One'. The 'first Adam' and the 'second Adam'; the physical body and the spiritual body; the primal Form or Phantom of the physical body; Luciferic interference. The physical body of Jesus of Nazareth, the bearer of the Christ-Being.

Theosophical ideas have been inadequate, so far, for understanding the Mystery of Golgotha. The three streams of thought recalled — Greek, Buddhist, Hebrew. The Ego in man and the Christ-Being in Jesus of Nazareth.

Development of Ego-consciousness in man; the physical body the mirror for thought. Degeneration through Luciferic influence of the physical body, and of the Phantom; the consequences for the intellect and for the Ego-consciousness which was becoming progressively enfeebled up to the time of the Mystery of Golgotha. The perfect Phantom, risen from the grave, multiplies itself like a physical cell and becomes the spiritual body in man. The Mystery of Golgotha the rescue of the Ego-consciousness.

Distinguishing characteristics of the two Jesus-children. Zarathustra and Buddha. The human Ego and the Ego of the Nathan-child. Union of the Ego of Zarathustra with the Nathan-Jesus, from twelfth to thirtieth year. Effects of the presence of the Christ-Being, after the Baptism, upon the Phantom of the physical body of the Nathan-Jesus.

LECTURE I

The object of these lectures is to place before you an idea of
the Christ-Event in so far as it is connected with the historical appearance of the Christ in the person of Jesus of Nazareth.
So many questions of the spiritual life are bound up with
this subject that the choice of it will enable us to make a wide
survey of the realm of Spiritual Science and its mission, and
to discuss the significance of the Anthroposophical Movement
for the spiritual life of the present time. We shall also have
the opportunity of learning what the content of religion is.
And since this content must spring from the common heritage
of mankind, we shall seek to know it in its relation to the
deeper sources of religious life, and to what the sources of
occult science have to tell us concerning the foundation of
all religious and philosophic endeavours. Much that we shall
have to discuss will seem to lie very far from the theme itself,
but it will all lead us back to our main purpose.

We shall best come to a more precise understanding of our
subject—modern religious life on the one hand and the
spiritual-scientific deepening of spiritual life on the other—if
we glance at the origins both of religious life and of occult
spiritual life in recent centuries. For as regards spiritual
development in Europe during this period, we can discern
two directions of thought which have been cultivated with
the utmost intensity: on the one hand an exaggeration of the
Jesus-Principle, and on the other a most careful, conscien-
tious preservation of the Christ-Principle. When we place
before our minds these two recent streams, we must see in the
exaggeration of the Jesus-Principle a great and dangerous
error in the spiritual life of those times, and on the other side
a movement of deep significance, a movement which seeks

above all the true paths and is careful to avoid the paths of error. From the outset, therefore, in our judgment of two entirely different spiritual movements, we have to ascribe serious errors to one of them and most earnest efforts after truth to the other.

The movement which interests us in connection with our spiritual-scientific point of view, and which we may call an extraordinarily dangerous error in a certain sense, is the movement known in the external world as Jesuitism. In Jesuitism we encounter a dangerous exaggeration of the Jesus-Principle. In the other movement, which for centuries has existed in Europe as Rosicrucianism, we have an inward Christ-movement which above all seeks carefully for the ways of truth.

Ever since a Jesuitical current arose in Europe, much has been said and written in exoteric life about Jesuitism. Those who wish to study spiritual life from its deeper sources will thus be concerned to see how far Jesuitism signifies a dangerous exaggeration of the Jesus-Principle. If we wish to arrive at a true characterisation of Jesuitism, we must get to know how the three chief principles of world-evolution, which are indicated in the most varied ways in the different world-outlooks, find practical expression in human life, including exoteric life. To-day we will first of all turn quite away from the deeper significance and characterisation of these three fundamental streams, which run through all life and all evolution, and will review them from an external point of view.

First of all we have the cognitional element in our soul-life. Now, whatever may be said against the abstractions of a one-sided intellectual search for truth, or against the alienation from life of many scientific, philosophical and theosophical endeavours, anyone who is clear in his own mind as to what he wills and what he can will, knows that Cognition belongs to the most deeply rooted activities of the soul. For whether we seek knowledge chiefly through thinking, or more through sensation or feeling, Cognition always signifies a taking account of the world around us, and also of ourselves. Hence we must say that whether we are satisfied for the moment with the simplest experiences of the soul, or whether we wish to devote ourselves to the most complicated analysis of the mysteries of existence, Cognition is the primary and most significant question. For it is basically through Cognition that we form a picture of the content of the world—a picture we live by and from which our entire soul-life is nourished. The very first sense-impression, in fact all sense-life, must be included in the realm of Cognition, along with the highest formulations of the intellect.

Under Cognition we must include also the impulse to distinguish between the beautiful and the ugly, for although it is true in a certain sense that there is no disputing about taste, yet cognition is involved when someone has adopted a certain judgment in a question of taste and can distinguish between the beautiful and the ugly. Again, our moral impulses—those which prompt us to do good and abstain from evil—must be seen as moral ideas, as cognition, or as impulses to do the one and avoid the other. Even what we call our conscience, however vague the impulses from it may be, comes under the heading of cognition. In short, the world we are consciously aware of, whether it be reality or maya; the world we live in consciously, everything we are conscious of—all this can be embraced under the heading: cognitive spiritual life.

Everyone, however, must acknowledge that under the surface of this cognitive life something else can be discerned; that in our everyday existence our soul-life gives evidence of many things which are not part of our conscious life. When we wake up in the morning, our soul-life is always strengthened and refreshed and newly born from sleep. During the unconsciousness of sleep we have gained something which is outside the realm of conscious cognition, but comes from a region where our soul is active below the level of consciousness.

In waking life, too, we must admit that we are impelled by impulses, instincts and forces which throw up their waves into our conscious life, while they work and have their being below it. We become aware that they work below the conscious when they rise above the surface which separates the conscious from the subconscious. And indeed our moral life also makes us aware of a subconscious soul-life of this kind, for we can see how in the moral realm this or that ideal comes to birth. It takes only a little self-knowledge to realise that these ideals do rise up into our soul-life, but that we are far from always knowing how our great moral ideals are connected with the deepest questions of existence, or how they belong to the will of God, in which they must ultimately be grounded. We might indeed compare our soul-life in its totality with a deep ocean. The depths of this oceanic soul-life throw up waves to the surface, and those that break out into the realm of air, which we can compare with normal consciousness, are brought within the range of conscious cognition. All conscious life is rooted in a subconscious soul-life.

Fundamentally, the whole evolution of mankind can be understood only if a subconscious soul-life of this kind is acknowledged. For what does the progress of spiritual life signify save that many things which have long dwelt down below take form for the first time when they are brought to surface level? So it is, for example, when an inventive idea arises in the form of an impulse towards discovery. Subconscious soul-life, as real as our conscious life, must therefore be recognised as a second element in our life of soul.

If we place this subconscious soul-life in a realm that is at first unknown—but not unknowable—we must contrast it with a third element. This element is immediately apparent to external, exoteric observation, for if we turn our attention to the outer world through our senses, or approach it through our intellect or any form of mental activity, we come to know all sorts of things. But a more exact consideration of every age of cognition compels us to realise that behind everything we can know about the world at large something else lies hidden: something that is certainly not unknowable but in every epoch has to be described as not yet known. And this not-yet-known, which lies below the surface of the known in the mineral, plant and animal kingdoms, belongs as much to ourselves as it does to external nature. It belongs to us in so far as we absorb and work up in our physical organism the materials and forces of the outer world; and inasmuch as we have within us a portion of nature, we have also within us a portion of the unknown in nature. So in the world wherein we live we must distinguish a triad: our conscious spiritual life; our subconscious soul-life below the threshold of consciousness; and that which, as the unknown in nature and at the same time in man, lives in us as part of the great unknown Nature.

This triad emerges directly from a rational observation of the world. And if looking away from all dogmatic statements, from all philosophical or theosophical traditions, in so far as these are clothed in conceptual definitions or formulations, we may ask: How has the human mind always expressed the the fact that this triad is present not only in the immediate environment, but in the whole world to which man himself belongs? We must then reply: Man gives the name of Spirit to all that can be known within the horizon of the conscious. He designates as the Son or the Logos that which works in the subconscious and throws up only its waves from down below. And to that which belongs equally to the unknown in Nature, and to the part of our own being which is of one kind with Nature, the name of the Father-Principle has always been given, because it was felt to express the relation of the third principle to the other two.

Besides what has now been said concerning the Spirit, the Son and the Father-Principle, it can be taken for granted that other differentiations we have formerly made, and also the differentiations made in this or that philosophy, have their justifications. But we can say that the most widely accepted idea of this differentiation corresponds with the account of it given here.

Now let us ask: How can we characterise the transition from that which belongs to the Spirit, and so plays directly into the conscious life of the soul, to the subconscious element which belongs to the Son-Principle? We shall best grasp this transition if we realise that into ordinary human consciousness there plays quite distinctly the element we designate as Will, in contrast to the elements of ideation and feeling. If we rightly interpret the Bible saying, 'The Spirit is willing, but the flesh is weak', it indicates that everything grasped by consciousness lies in the realm of the Spirit, whereas by 'the flesh' is meant everything that lies more in the subconscious. As to the nature of the Will, we need only think of that which plays up from the subconscious and enters into our consciousness only when we form concepts of it. Only when we transform into concepts and ideas the dark impelling forces which are rooted in the elemental part of the soul—only then do they enter the realm of the Spirit; otherwise they remain in the realm of the Son-Principle. And since the Will plays through our feelings into the life of ideas, we see quite clearly the breaking out into the conscious of the waves from the subconscious ocean. In our threefold soul-life we have two elements, ideation and feeling, which belong to conscious life, but feeling descends directly into the realm of the Will, and the nearer we come to the impulses of Will, the further we descend into the subconscious, the dark realms into which we sink completely when consciousness is engulfed in deep, dreamless sleep.

Thus we see that the Will-element, because it descends into the realm of the subconscious, stands towards the individual being of man in a relationship quite different from that of cognition, the realm of the Spirit. And so, when we differentiate between Spirit and Son, we may be impelled to surmise that man's relationship to the Spirit is different from his relationship to the Son. How is this to be understood?

Even in exoteric life it is quite easy to understand. Certainly the realm of cognition has given rise to all kinds of debate, but if people would only come to understand one another concerning the concepts and ideas they formulate for themselves, controversy over questions of cognition would gradually cease. I have often emphasised that we no longer dispute over mathematics, because we have raised mathematics entirely into consciousness. The things we dispute about are those not yet raised into consciousness: we still allow our subconscious impulses, instincts and passions to play into them. So we see that in the realm of cognition we have to do with something more universally human than anything to be found in the subconscious realm. When we meet another human being and enter into the most varied relationships with him, it is in the realm of conscious spiritual life that understanding should be possible. And a mark of a healthy soul-life is that it will always wish and hope to reach an understanding with the other person concerning things that belong to conscious spiritual life. It will be unhealthy for the soul if that hope is lost.

On the other hand, we must recognise the Will-element, and everything in another person's subconscious, as something which should on no account be intruded upon; it must be regarded as his innermost sanctuary. We need consider only how unpleasant to a healthy soul-life is the feeling that the Will of another man is being put under compulsion. It is not only aesthetically but morally unpleasant to see the conscious soul-life of anyone eliminated by hypnotism or any other powerful means; or to see the will-power of one person working directly on the Will of another. The only healthy way to gain influence over another person's Will is through cognition. Cognition should be the means whereby one soul comes to an understanding with another. A person must first translate his wishes into a conceptual form; then they may influence another person's cognition, and they should touch his Will only by this indirect route. Nothing else can be satisfactory in the highest, most ideal sense to a healthy life of soul. Every kind of forcible working of Will upon Will must evoke an unpleasant impression.

In other words, human nature strives, in so far as it is healthy, to develop in the realm of the Spirit the life it has in common with others, and to cherish and respect the realm of the subconscious, in so far as it comes to expression in the human organism, as an inviolable sanctuary that should rest in the personality, the individuality, of each man and should not be approached save through the door of conscious cognition. So at least a modern consciousness, attuned to our epoch, must feel if it is to know itself to be healthy.

In later lectures we shall see whether this was so in all periods of human evolution. What has been said to-day will help us to think clearly about what is outside us and what is within us, at least for our own period. This leads to the conclusion that fundamentally the realm of the Son— embracing everything that we designate as the Son or Logos—must be awakened in each individual as a quite personal concern; and that the realm of common life, where men may be influenced by one another, is the realm of the Spirit.

We see this expressed in the grandest, most significant way in the New Testament accounts of the attitude of Christ Jesus towards His first disciples and followers. From all that is told concerning the Christ-Event we can gather that the followers who had hastened to Jesus during his lifetime were bewildered when His life ended with the crucifixion; with that form of death which, in the land where the Christ-Event took its course, was regarded as the only possible expiation for the greatest crimes. And although this death on the cross did not affect everyone as it did Saul,

who later became Paul, and as Saul had concluded that
someone who suffered such a death could not be the Messiah,
or the Christ—for the crucifixion had made a milder
impression on the disciples, one might say—yet it is obvious
that the writers of the Gospels wished to give the impression
that Christ Jesus, through his subjection to the shameful
death on the cross, had forfeited some of the effect he had had
on the hearts of those around him.

But with this account something else is connected. The
influence that Christ Jesus had acquired—an influence we
must characterise more exactly during these lectures—was
restored to Him after the Resurrection. Whatever may be
our present thoughts about the Resurrection, we shall have
to discuss it here in the light of occult science; and then, if
we simply go by the Gospel narratives, one thing will be
clear: for those to whom Christ appeared after the Resurrection He had become someone who was present in a
quite special way, different entirely from His previous
presence.

In speaking on the Gospel of St. John I have already
pointed out how impossible it would have been for anyone
who knew Jesus not to recognise Him after three days, or to
confuse Him with someone else, if He had not appeared in an
altered form. The Evangelists wish particularly to evoke the
impression that the Christ appeared in this altered form.
But they also wish to indicate something else. For the Christ
to exert influence on human souls, a certain receptivity in
those souls was necessary. And this receptivity had to be
acted on not merely by an influence from the realm of the
Spirit but by the actual sight of the Christ-Being.

If we ask what this signifies, we must realise that when a
person stands before us, his effect upon us goes beyond anything we are conscious of. Whenever a human being or other
being works upon us, unconscious elements affect our soul-
life; they are produced by the other being indirectly through
consciousness, but he can produce them only if he stands

before us in actuality. What the Christ brought about from person to person after the so-called Resurrection was something that worked up from the unconscious soul-powers of the disciples into their soul-life: an acquaintance with the Son. Hence the differences in the portrayal of the risen Christ; hence, too, the variations in the accounts, showing how the Christ appeared to one or other person, according to the disposition of the person concerned. Here we see the Christ-Being acting on the subconscious part of the souls of the disciples; hence the appearances are quite individual, and we should not complain because they are not uniform.

If, however, the significance of the Christ for the world was to be His bringing to all men something common to all of them, then not only this individual working of the Son had to proceed from the Christ, but the element of Spirit, which can encompass something that belongs to all men, had to be renewed by Him. This is indicated by the statement that after the Christ had worked upon the Logos-nature of man, He sent forth the Spirit in the form of the renewed or 'Holy Spirit'. Thus was created that element common to all men which is characterised when we are told that the disciples, after they had received the Spirit, began to speak in the most diverse tongues. Here we are shown how the common element resides in the outpouring of the Holy Spirit. And something else is indicated: how different is this outpouring of the Spirit from the simple imparting of the power of the Son, for in the Acts of the Apostles we are told that certain persons to whom the apostles came had already received the Jesus-baptism, and yet they had now to receive for the first time the Spirit, symbolically indicated by the laying on of hands. In the characterisation of the Christ-Event we are made very precisely aware of the difference between the working we have to designate as the Christ-working, which acts upon the subconscious impulses of the soul and so must have a personal, inward character, and the

Spirit-element, which represents something common to all mankind.

It is this Spirit-element that those who have named themselves 'Rosicrucians' have sought to preserve most carefully, as far as human weakness permits. The Rosicrucians have always wished to adhere strictly to the rule that even in the highest regions of Initiation nothing must be worked upon except the Spirit-element which, as common between man and man, is available in the evolution of humanity. The Initiation of the Rosicrucians was an Initiation of the Spirit. It was never an Initiation of the Will, for the Will of man was to be respected as a sanctuary in the innermost part of the soul. Hence the individual was led to those Initiations which were to take him beyond the stage of Imagination, Inspiration and Intuition, but always so that he could recognise within himself the response which the development of the Spirit-element was to call forth. No influence was to be exerted on the Will.

We must not mistake this attitude for one of indifference towards the Will. The point is that by excluding all direct working upon the Will, the purest spiritual influence was imparted indirectly through the Spirit. When we come to an understanding with another man with regard to entering on the path of knowledge of the Spirit, light and warmth are radiated from the spiritual path, and they then enkindle the Will, but always by the indirect path through the Spirit— never otherwise.

In Rosicrucianism, therefore, we can observe in the highest sense that impulse of Christianity which finds twofold expression: on the one hand in the Son-element, in the Christ-working which goes down deeply into the subconscious; on the other, in the Spirit-working which embraces all that falls within the horizon of our consciousness. We must indeed bear the Christ in our Will; but the way in which men should come to an understanding with each other in life concerning the Christ can be found only—

in the Rosicrucian sense—through a conscious soul-life which penetrates ever more deeply into the occult.

In reaction against many other spiritual streams in Europe, the opposite way was taken by those who are usually called Jesuits. The radical, fundamental difference between what we justifiably call the Christian way of the Spirit and the Jesuit way of the Spirit, which gives a one-sided exaggeration to the Jesus-Principle, is that the intention of the Jesuit way is to work *directly*, at all times, upon the Will. The difference is clearly shown in the method by which the pupil of Jesuitism is educated. Jesuitism is not to be taken lightly, or merely exoterically, but also esoterically, for it is rooted in esotericism. It is not, however, rooted in the spiritual life that is poured out through the symbol of Pentecost, but it seeks to root itself directly in the Jesus-element of the Son, which means in the Will; and thereby it exaggerates the Jesus-element of the Will.

This will be seen when we now enquire into the esoteric part of Jesuitism, its various spiritual exercises. How were these exercises arranged? The essential point is that every single pupil of Jesuitism goes through exercises which lead into the occult life, but into the Will, and within the field of occultism they hold the Will in severe discipline; they 'break it in', one might say. And the significant fact is that this discipline of the Will does not arise merely from the surface of life, but from something deeper, because the pupil has been led into the occult, in the way just indicated.

If now, leaving aside the exercises of prayer preparatory to all Jesuit exercises, we consider these occult exercises, at least in their chief points, we find that the pupil has first to call up a vivid Imagination of Christ Jesus as the King of the Worlds—mark this carefully: an Imagination. And no one would be received into the degrees of Jesuitism who had not gone through such exercises, and had not experienced in his soul the transformation which such psychic exercises mean for the whole man. But this Imaginative presentation of

Christ Jesus as King of the Worlds has to be preceded by
something else. The pupil has to call up for himself, in
absolute solitude and seclusion, a picture of man as he was
created in the world, and how by falling into sin he incurred
the possibility of most terrible punishments. And it is
strictly prescribed how one must picture such a man; how if
he were left to himself he would incur the utmost of torturing
penalties. The rules are extraordinarily severe. With all
other concepts or ideas excluded, this picture must live
uninterruptedly within the soul of the future Jesuit, the
picture of the Godforsaken man, the man exposed to the
most fearful punishments, together with the feeling: 'That
am I, since I have come into the world and have forsaken
God, and have exposed myself to the possibility of the most
fearful punishments.' This must call forth the fear of being
forsaken by God, and detestation of man as he is according
to his own nature.

Then, in a further Imagination, over against the picture
of the outcast, God-forsaken man, must be set the picture of
the God full of pity who then became Christ, and through
His acts on earth atones for what man has brought about by
forsaking the divine path. In contrast to the Imagination of
the God-forsaken man, there must arise that of the all-
merciful, loving Being, Christ Jesus, to whom alone it is
due that man is not exposed to all possible punishments
working upon his soul. And, just as vividly as a feeling of
contempt for the forsaking of the divine path had first to
become fixed in the soul of the Jesuit pupil, so must a feeling
of humility and contrition now take hold of him in the
presence of Christ.

When these two feelings have been called forth in the
pupil, then for several weeks he has to practise severe
exercises, picturing to himself in Imagination all details of
the life of Jesus from his birth to the Crucifixion and Resurrection. And all that can arise in the soul emerges when the
pupil lives in rigorous seclusion and, except for necessary

meals, lets nothing else work upon his soul than the pictures which the Gospels give of the compassionate life of Jesus. But these pictures do not merely appear before him in thoughts and ideas; they must work upon his soul in vivid, living Imaginations.

Only someone who really knows how the human soul is transformed through Imaginations which work with full living power—only he knows that under such conditions the soul is in fact completely changed. Such Imaginations, because they are concentrated in the most intense, one-sided way, first on sinful man, secondly on the compassionate God, and then only on the pictures from the New Testament, evoke precisely, through the law of polarity, a strengthened Will. These pictures produce their effect directly, at first hand, for any reflection upon them must be dutifully excluded. It is solely a matter of holding before one's mind these Imaginations, as they have just been described.

What then follows is this. In the further exercises Christ Jesus—and now we may no longer say *Christ* but exclusively *Jesus*—is represented as the universal King of the Worlds, and thereby the Jesus element is exaggerated. Because Christ had to be incarnated in a human body, the purely spiritual took part in the physical world; but over against this participation stand the monumental and most significant words: 'My kingdom is not of this world.' We can exaggerate the Jesus element by making Jesus into a king of this world, by making Him that which He would have become if He had not resisted the tempter who wished to give Him 'all the kingdoms of the world and the glory thereof'. Then Jesus of Nazareth would have been a king who, unlike other kings who possess only a portion of the earth, would have had the whole earth under his sway. If we think of this king portrayed in this guise, his kingly power so increased that the whole earth is his domain, then we should have the very picture that followed the other exercises through which the personal will of each Jesuit pupil had been sufficiently strengthened.

To prepare for this picture of 'King Jesus', this Ruler over all the kingdoms of the earth, the pupil had to form an Imagination of Babylon and the plain around Babylon as a living picture, and, enthroned over Babylon, Lucifer with his banner. This picture had to be visualised with great exactitude, for it is a powerful Imagination: King Lucifer, with his banner and his hosts of Luciferic angels, seated amidst fire and dense smoke, as he sends out his angels to conquer the kingdoms of the earth. And the whole danger that issues from the 'banner of Lucifer' must first of all be imagined by itself, without casting a glance upon Christ Jesus. The soul must be entirely engrossed in the Imagination of the danger which issues from the banner of Lucifer. The soul must learn to feel that the greatest danger to the world's existence that could be conjured forth would be a victory for the banner of Lucifer. And when this picture has had its effect, the other Imagination, 'The banner of Jesus', must take its place. The pupil must now visualise Jerusalem and the plain around Jerusalem; King Jesus with His hosts, how He sends out His hosts, how He conquers and drives off the hosts of Lucifer and makes Himself King of the whole earth—the victory of the banner of Jesus over the banner of Lucifer.

These are the strength-giving Imaginations for the Will which are brought before the soul of the Jesuit pupil. This is what completely changes his Will; makes him such that in his Will, because it is trained occultly, he turns away from everything else and surrenders absolutely to the idea: 'King Jesus must become the Ruler upon earth, and we who belong to His army have to employ every means to make Him Ruler of the earth. To this we pledge ourselves, we who belong to His host assembled on the plain of Jerusalem, against the host of Lucifer assembled on the plain of Babylon. And the greatest disgrace for a soldier of King Jesus is to forsake His banner.'

These ideas, gathered up into a single resolution of the Will, can certainly give the Will immense strength. But we must ask: what is it in the soul-life that has been directly attacked? The element that ought to be regarded as intrinsically holy, the element that ought not to be touched—the Will-element. In so far as this Jesuit training lays hold of the Will-element, while the Jesus-idea seizes the Will-element completely, in so far is the concept of the dominion of Jesus exaggerated in the most dangerous way—dangerous because through it the Will becomes so strong that it can work directly upon the Will of another. For where the Will becomes so strong through Imaginations, which means by occult methods, it acquires the capacity for working directly upon the Will of another, and hence also along all the other occult paths to which such a Will can have recourse.

Thus we see how in recent centuries we encounter these two movements, among many others: one has exaggerated the Jesus-element and sees in 'King Jesus' the sole ideal of Christianity, while the other looks solely at the Christ-element and carefully sets aside anything that could go beyond it. This second outlook has been much calumniated because it maintains that Christ has sent the Spirit, so that, indirectly through the Spirit, Christ can enter into the hearts and minds of men. In the development of civilisation during the last few centuries there is hardly a greater contrast than that between Jesuitism and Rosicrucianism, for Jesuitism contains nothing of what Rosicrucianism regards as the highest ideal concerning human worth and human dignity, while Rosicrucianism has always sought to guard itself from any influence which could in the remotest sense be called Jesuitical.

In this lecture I wished to show how even so lofty an element as the Jesus-principle can be exaggerated and then becomes dangerous, and how necessary it is to sink oneself into the depths of the Christ-Being if we wish to understand how the strength of Christianity must reside in esteeming, to the very highest degree, human dignity and human worth, and in strictly refraining from groping our clumsy way into man's inmost sanctuary. Rosicrucianism, even more than Christian mysticism, is attacked by the Jesuit element, because the Jesuits feel that true Christianity is being sought elsewhere than in the setting which offers merely 'King Jesus' in the leading role. But the Imaginations here indicated, together with the prescribed exercises, have made the Will so strong that even protests brought against it in the name of the Spirit can be defeated.

LECTURE II

Yesterday I tried to give you a picture of a form of Initiation which ought not to exist, according to our valuation of human nature. This Initiation, as we have seen it in Jesuitism, leads to the acquisition of certain occult faculties, but if we bring a cleansed and purified occult vision to bear upon these faculties, they cannot be considered good. It will now be my task to show that the Rosicrucian way is characterised by all that high regard for human nature which we recognise as equally our own. But we must first be clear on certain points.

From explanations given previously in various forms, we know that the Rosicrucian Initiation is essentially a development of the Christian Initiation, so that we can speak of it as a Christian-Rosicrucian Initiation. In earlier lecture-courses the purely Christian Initiation, with its seven degrees, and the Rosicrucian Initiation, also with seven degrees, have been compared. But now we must note that with regard to Initiation the principle of the progress of the human soul must be strictly maintained.

We know that the Rosicrucian Initiation had its proper beginning somewhere about the thirteenth century. At that time it was recognised by those individualities who have to guide the deeper destinies of human evolution as the right Initiation for the more advanced human souls. This shows that the Initiation of the Rose-Cross takes full account of the continuous progress of the human soul and must therefore pay particular attention to the fact that since the thirteenth century the human soul has developed further. Souls which are to be led to Initiation in our day can no longer adopt the standpoint of the thirteenth century. I want especially to point this out because in our time there is such a strong desire to label everything with some mark or other, with some catchword. From this bad habit, and not for any justified reason, our anthroposophical movement has been given a label which could lead gradually to something like a calamity.

It is true that within our movement the principle of Rosicrucianism can be found in all completeness, so that we can penetrate into the sources of Rosicrucianism. So it is that persons who by means of our anthroposophical training penetrate into these sources can properly call themselves Rosicrucians. But it must be emphasised just as strongly that outsiders have no right to designate as Rosicrucian the anthroposophical stream we represent, simply because our movement has been given—consciously or unconsciously—an entirely false label. We are no longer standing where the Rosicrucians stood in the thirteenth century and on through the following centuries, for we take into account the progress of the human soul. Hence the way indicated in my book, *Knowledge of the Higher Worlds*, as the way best adapted for gaining access to the Higher Worlds must not without further explanation be equated with what may be called the Rosicrucian way. Through our movement we can penetrate into true Rosicrucianism, but our movement extends over a far wider domain, for it embraces the whole of Theosophy; hence it should not be labelled Rosicrucian. Our movement must be described simply as the spiritual science of to-day, the anthroposophical spiritual science of the twentieth century. Outsiders, particularly, will fall—more or less unconsciously—into some kind of misunderstanding if they describe our movement simply as Rosicrucian. But an outstanding achievement of Rosicrucianism since the dawn of modern spiritual life in the thirteenth century has been to establish a rule which must also be ours: the rule that all modern Initiation in the deepest sense of the word must recognise and treasure the independence of the most holy element in man's inner life, his Will-centre, as indicated yesterday. The occult methods there described are designed to overcome and enslave the human will and to set it on a predetermined course; hence a true occultism will rigorously avoid them.

Before characterising Rosicrucianism and present-day Initiation, we must mention a decisively relevant point: the Rosicrucianism of the thirteenth, fourteenth and even of the sixteenth and seventeenth centuries has again had to be modified for our time. The Rosicrucianism of those earlier centuries could not reckon with a spiritual element which has since entered into human evolution. Without this element to-day we can no longer understand rightly the fundamentals of all those spiritual streams which arise from the ground of occultism, including therefore any theosophical stream. For reasons we shall see more exactly in the course of these lectures, the teaching of reincarnation and karma, of repeated earth-lives, was excluded for many centuries from the external, exoteric teachings of Christianity. In the thirteenth century the teaching of reincarnation and karma had not yet entered, in the highest sense, into the first stages of Rosicrucian initiation. One could go far, up to the fourth or fifth degree; one could go through what was called the Rosicrucian studium—the acquiring of Imagination, the reading of the occult script, the finding of the philosopher's stone—and one could experience something of what is called the mystical death. One could reach this stage and acquire exceptionally high occult knowledge, but without needing to achieve full clarity concerning the illuminating teachings of reincarnation and karma.

We must be clear that human thinking progresses and now embraces forms of thought which, if only we follow them out logically—and this can easily be done on the external, exoteric level—lead unconditionally to a recognition of repeated earth-lives and so to the idea of karma. The words spoken through the lips of Strader in my second

Rosicrucian drama, *The Soul's Probation*, are absolutely true: namely that a logical thinker to-day, if he is not to break with everything that the thought-forms of the last century have brought in, must come finally to a recognition of karma and reincarnation.

This is something deeply rooted in present-day spiritual life. Just because this knowledge has been slowly prepared and has these deep roots, it emerges little by little, as though independently, in the West. It is indeed remarkable how the necessity of recognising repeated earth-lives has independently made itself felt—though certainly only by outstanding individual thinkers. We need only call attention to certain facts which are quite forgotten, intentionally or unintentionally, in our present-day literature. Take, for example, what comes out so wonderfully in Lessing's *Education of the Human Race*. We see how Lessing, that great mind of the eighteenth century who at the zenith of his life gathered up his thoughts and wrote the *Education of the Human Race*, came as though by inspiration to the thought of repeated earth-lives. So does the idea of repeated earth-lives find its way, as though by inner necessity, into modern life. It has to be taken into consideration, but certainly not in the way that ideas of this kind are considered in our history books or in cultured circles nowadays. For in such cases resort is had to the familiar formula that when a clever man grows old, excuses must be made for him. So it is said that although we may appreciate Lessing in his earlier works, we must allow that in later years, when he came to the idea of repeated earth-lives, he had become somewhat feeble.

In more recent times the idea occurs sporadically. Drossbach, a nineteenth-century psychologist, spoke of it in the only way then possible. Without occultism, simply by observing nature, he tried in his own way as a psychologist to establish the idea of repeated earth-lives. Again, in the middle of the last century, a small society offered a prize for the best essay on the immortality of the soul. This was a remarkable occurrence in German spiritual life, and is very little known. Moreover, the prize went to an essay by Widenmann which tried to prove the immortality of the soul in the sense of repeated earth-lives: certainly an imperfect attempt, but it could not be otherwise in the fifties of the last century, when the necessary thought-forms had not developed far enough. One could quote various other instances where the idea of repeated earth-lives springs up, as though in response to a postulate, a demand, of the nineteenth century. Hence in my little book, *Reincarnation and Karma*, and also in my book, *Theosophy*, the ideas of repeated earth-lives and of karma could be worked out in relation to the thought-forms of natural science, but with reference to human individuality in contrast to the animal species.

We must, however, be clear on one essential point: there is an immense difference between the way in which Western men have come to this idea simply through thinking, and the way in which it figures in Buddhism, for instance. It is most interesting to see how Lessing came to the idea of repeated earth-lives. The result can of course be compared with the idea of repeated earth-lives in Buddhism, and even given the same name; but the way taken by Lessing is very different and is not generally known. How did he come to this idea?

We can see this quite clearly if we go through the *Education of the Human Race*. There is no doubt that human evolution gives evidence of progress in the strictest sense. Lessing argued that this progress is an education of humanity by the Divine Powers. God gave into men's hands a first elementary book, the Old Testament. Thereby a certain stage of evolution was achieved. When the human race had gone further, it was given the second elementary book, the New Testament. And then Lessing sees in our time something that goes beyond the New Testament: an independent feeling in the human soul for the true, the good and the beautiful. This marks for him a third stage in the education of the human race. The thought of the education of mankind by the Divine Powers is worked out in a lofty style.

Lessing then asks himself: What is the one and only way to explain this progress? He cannot explain it otherwise than by allowing every soul to participate in each epoch of human evolution, if human progress is to have any meaning at all. For it would have no meaning if one soul lived only in the epoch of Old Testament civilisation and another soul only in the New Testament epoch. It has meaning only if souls are taken through all the epochs of civilisation and share in all the stages of human education. In other words, if the soul lives through repeated earth-lives, the progressive education of the human race makes good sense. So the idea of repeated earth-lives springs up in Lessing's mind as something that belongs to human destiny.

In a deeper sense the following underlies his thinking. If a soul was incarnated at the time of the Old Testament, it took into itself whatever it could take; when it reappears in a later time it carries the fruits of its previous life into the next life, and the fruits of that life into the one following, and so on. Thus the successive stages of evolution are interlocked. And whatever a soul achieves is achieved not only for itself, but for all mankind. Humanity is a great organism, and for Lessing reincarnation is necessary in order that the whole human race can progress. Thus it is historical evolution, the concern of humanity as a whole, that he takes as his starting-point, and from there he is impelled to a recognition of reincarnation.

It is different if we trace out the same idea in Buddhism. There, a person is concerned merely with himself, with his own psyche. The individual says to himself: I am placed in the world of maya; desire brought me into it, and in the course of repeated incarnations I shall free myself as an individual soul from the necessity of living again on earth. This applies to the single individual; all the attention is centred on him. That is the great difference.

Whether a person looks at the process from within, as in Buddhism, or from without, as Lessing does, his gaze takes in the whole of human evolution. In both cases the same idea emerges, but in the West the path to it is quite different. While the Buddhist limits himself to concern for the individual, the man of the West is concerned with the whole of humanity. He feels himself bound up with all men as a single organism.

What is it that has taught Western man the necessity of realising, above all, that his concern is with all mankind? The reason is that into the sphere of the heart, into his world of feeling, he has received the words of Christ Jesus concerning human brotherhood: that it is beyond all nationality, beyond all racial characteristics, and that humanity is a great organism.

Hence it is interesting to see how Drossbach, although his thinking is still imperfect, because the scientific ideas of the first half of the nineteenth century had not yet produced the corresponding thought-forms, does not take the Buddhistic path, but a universal cosmic one. Drossbach starts from the thoughts of natural science and observes the soul in its cosmic aspect. He cannot think otherwise of the soul than as a seed which goes through an external form and reappears in other external forms, and so is reincarnated. With him, this idea turns into fantasy, for he thinks that the world itself must be transformed, whereas Lessing thought correctly of short periods of time. Widenmann, too, in his prize essay, brings the immortality of the soul into logical connection with the question of reincarnation.

So we see that these ideas appear quite sporadically, and it is right that in spite of faulty modes of thinking they should spring up in minds such as these, and in others also. The great evolutionary change which the human soul has undergone from the eighteenth to the twentieth century is such that everyone to-day who begins the study of world progress must above all assimilate those thought-forms which lead quite naturally to the acceptance and making credible of the ideas of reincarnation and karma. Between the thirteenth and eighteenth centuries human thought was not sufficiently advanced to come by itself to a recognition of reincarnation. One has always to start from the stage reached by the most highly developed thought of the period. To-day the starting point must be that form of thinking which, on the basis of natural science, regards the idea of repeated earth-lives as logical—which means hypothetically true. So do the times advance.

Without describing the Rosicrucian path in detail to-day, we will bring out what is essential both to it and to the way of knowledge at the present time. The characteristic of both is that everyone who gives advice and guidance for Initiation will value in the deepest sense the independence and inviolability of the sphere of the human Will. Hence the essential point is that through a special kind of moral and spiritual culture the ordinary interweaving of the physical body, etheric body, astral body and ego must be changed. And those directions which are given for the training of the moral feelings, as also those for concentration in thinking, for meditation—all this makes finally for the one goal of loosening the spiritual texture which binds together the physical and etheric bodies, so that the etheric body does not remain so firmly fitted into the physical body as it naturally is. All the exercises strive after this lifting out, this loosening, of the etheric body. Thereby another union between the astral body and the etheric body is brought about. It is because in ordinary life the etheric body and the physical body are so firmly united that the astral body cannot normally feel or experience what is going on in the etheric body. Because the etheric body has its seat within the physical body, our astral body and our ego perceive only what the physical body brings them from the world and enables them to think of through the instrument of the brain. The etheric body is too deeply embedded in the physical body for it to be experienced in ordinary life as an independent entity, as an independent instrument of cognition, or as an instrument of feeling and willing.

The efforts in concentrated thinking, according to the instructions given nowadays—and given also by the Rosicrucians—the efforts in meditation, the cleansing of the moral feelings: all these finally produce on the etheric body the effect described in my book, *Knowledge of the Higher Worlds.* As we use our eyes for seeing and our hands for grasping, so eventually we shall use the etheric body with its organs, but for looking into the spiritual, not the physical, world. The way in which we gather together and concentrate our inner life works for the independence of the etheric body.

It is necessary, however, that we should first permeate ourselves, at least tentatively, with the idea of karma. And we do this when we establish a certain moral equilibrium, a balance of the soul-forces of feeling. A person who cannot to a certain extent grasp the thought that 'in the long run I myself am to blame for my impulses', will not be able to make good progress. A certain equanimity and understanding with regard to karma, even if only a purely hypothetical understanding, are necessary as a starting-point. A person who never gets away from his ego, who is so dependent upon his narrowly limited ways of feeling and perception that when things go wrong he always blames others and never himself; a person who is always filled with the idea that the world, or a part of his environment, is against him; a man who never gets beyond the results of applying ordinary thinking to whatever can be learnt from exoteric Theosophy —such a person will find progress particularly difficult. Hence it is well that in order to develop equanimity and calmness of soul we should make ourselves familiar with the idea that when something does not succeed, particularly on the occult path, we must blame not others but ourselves. This does most to help our progress. What helps least is

always wanting to lay the blame on the world outside, or
always wanting to change our training methods.

Our attitude in such matters is more important than perhaps appears. It is better to test carefully, at all times, how
little we have learnt, and to seek the fault in ourselves when
progress is not made. It is a quite significant advance when
we can make up our minds always to seek the fault in ourselves. Then we shall see that we are making progress not
only in farther off things but also in matters of external life.
Those who have some experience in this field will always be
able to testify that by accepting the blame for their own
non-success, they have found something that makes precisely
their external life easy and bearable. We shall get on much
more easily with our environment when we can truly grasp
this fact. We shall rise above much grumbling and hypo-
chondria, above complaining and lamenting, and pursue our
way more calmly. For we should reflect that in every true
modern Initiation he who gives advice is under the strictest
obligation not to penetrate into the innermost sanctuary of
the soul. With regard to this most inward part of the soul,
therefore, we have from the start to undertake something for
ourselves, and we should not complain that we are perhaps
not getting the right advice. The advice may be right and
yet the results may not be satisfactory, if we fail to make the
resolve I have indicated.

This equanimity, this calmness, once we have made our
choice—and the choice should come only from a serious
resolve—is a good ground for meditation concerned with
thoughts and feelings. In everything founded on Rosicrucianism an important point is that in meditation and
concentration we are always directed not to dogma but to
the universally human. The deviation of which we spoke
yesterday takes its start from subject-matter that is first
given to the aspirant for holding in his mind. But what if this
subject-matter had first to be tested by occult cognition?
What if it were not in any way firmly established in

advance? We must take our stand on Rosicrucian principles, one of which is that we are not in a position to decide about anything which is supported only by external documents, for example, the accounts of what took place as the Event of Golgotha. We must come to know these things first by the occult path; we may not assume them beforehand. Hence we should start from the universally human, from that which can be justified by every soul.

A glance into the great world, marvelling at the revelation of light in the sun, feeling that what our eyes see of light is only the external veil of the light, its external revelation, or, as is said in Christian esotericism, the glory of light, and then yielding oneself up to the thought that behind the external sensible light something quite different is hidden— all this is fundamentally human. To think of, to gaze on, the light spread out through infinite space, and then clearly to feel that in this infinitely extended element of the light something spiritual must live, something which weaves this web of light in space; to concentrate upon these thoughts, to live in them—here we have something universally human, presented not through dogma but through universal feeling. Or again, to perceive the warmth of nature, to feel how through the universe, along with the warmth, something moves in which there is spirit. Then, out of certain relationships in our own organism with the feeling of love, to concentrate on the thought of how warmth can exist spiritually, how it lives pulsing through the world. Then, to sink oneself into what we can learn from intuitions given to us by modern occult teaching. Then to take counsel with those who know something in this realm as to concentrating in the right way upon world thoughts, cosmic thoughts. And further, the ennobling, the cleansing, of moral perceptions, whereby we come to understand that what we feel to be moral is reality. So we rise above the prejudice that these moral feelings are something transitory; we realise that they live on, are stamped into us as moral realities. We learn to feel the responsibility of being placed in the world as conscious beings, together with our moral feelings. All esoteric life is fundamentally directed towards universally human experiences of this kind.

I will now describe how far we can go through exercises which take their start in this way from human nature, if only we devote ourselves to a clear-sighted examination of our own human nature. From this beginning we come to a loosening of the connection between the physical body and the etheric body, and to a new kind of knowledge. We give birth as it were, to a second man within ourselves, so that we are no longer so firmly connected with the physical body as before. And in the finest moments of life we feel the etheric and astral bodies as though enclosed in an external sheath, and thereby know ourselves to be free from the instrument of the physical body. That is what we attain. We shall then be led to see our physical body in its true being, and to recognise how it affects us when we are within it. We become aware of the whole working of the physical body upon us only when we have in a certain sense come out of it, like the snake which after casting its skin can look upon the skin from outside, though feeling it as a part of itself. Through the first stages of Initiation we learn in like manner to feel ourselves free from the physical body, and learn to recognise it. At this moment quite special feelings will steal over us, which may be described as follows. (There are so many different experiences along the path of Initiation that it has not yet been possible to describe them all. In *Knowledge of the Higher Worlds* you will find much on the subject, but there is a great deal more.)

The first experience, open to nearly everyone who turns from ordinary life to pursue the path of knowledge, leads us to say, in accordance with our feeling: 'This physical body as it is, as it appears to me, has not been formed by myself. Most certainly I have not made this physical body, through which I have been brought to be what I am in the world. Without this body, the Ego which I now regard as my great ideal, would not have arisen within me. I have become what I am only through having kept my physical body riveted upon me.'

At first all this gives rise to something like resentment, bitterness, against the Cosmic Powers. It is easy to say, 'I will not cherish this resentment.' But when there arises before us in melancholy majesty a picture of what we have become through being bound up with the physical body, the effect is overwhelming. We feel something like bitter hatred for the Cosmic Powers on this account. But now our occult training must be so far advanced that we overcome this hatred and on a higher level can say with our whole being, with our individuality which has already come down into repeated incarnations, that we ourselves are responsible for what our physical body has become. When we have mastered the bitterness, we experience the perception, already often described: 'Now I know I am that very thing which appears there as the changed form of my physical being. That I am myself. But because my physical being was crushing me to death, I knew nothing of it.'

We stand here before the significant meeting with the Guardian of the Threshold. But if we come so far, if through the strenuousness of our exercises we experience what has just been said, then from out of what is common to human nature we recognise that we are as we are in our present form as the result of preceding incarnations. But we also recognise that we can experience the deepest pain and must work our way out beyond this pain to the overcoming of our present existence. And for every man who is sufficiently far advanced and has experienced these feelings in all their intensity, who has looked upon the Guardian of the Threshold, there arises of necessity an Imaginative picture, a picture not painted by constraint, as in Jesuitism, from passages in the Bible but a picture that each man experiences through having felt, in a general human sense, what he is. Through these experiences he will quite naturally come to know the picture of the Divine Ideal-Man, who like us lived in a physical body, and who like us in this physical body felt all that a physical body can bring about. The Temptation, and the picture of it as presented to us in the synoptic Gospels, the leading of Christ Jesus to the mountain, the promise of all external realities, the desire to cling to these outer realities, the temptation to remain attached to matter: in short, the temptation to remain with the Guardian of the Threshold and not to pass beyond him appears to us in the great Imaginative picture of Christ Jesus standing on the mountain, with the Tempter beside Him—a picture that would have arisen before us even if we had never heard of the Gospels. And then we know that he who wrote the story of the Temptation depicted his own experience of seeing, in the spirit, Christ Jesus and the Tempter. Then we know it is true in the Spirit that the writer of the Gospel has described something that we ourselves can experience even if we knew nothing of the Gospels. Thus we shall be led to a picture which is similar to the picture in the Gospels. We gain for ourselves what stands in the Gospels. Nothing is forced upon us; everything is drawn forth from the depths of our own nature. We proceed from the universally human and bring forth the Gospels afresh through our occult life. We feel ourselves at one with the writers of the Gospels.

Then there arises within us another feeling, a next step along the occult path. We feel how the Tempter has grown into a powerful Being who is behind all the phenomena of the world. Yes, we learn indeed to know the Tempter, but by degrees we learn in a certain way to value him. We learn to say: 'The world spread out before us, whether it be Maya or something else, has its right to exist; it has revealed something to me.' Then comes a second feeling, a quite definite one for every person who fulfils the conditions of a Rosicrucian initiation. The feeling arises: 'We belong to the Spirit Who lives in all things, and with Whom we have to reckon. We cannot in the least comprehend the Spirit if we do not surrender ourselves to it.' Then fear comes over us. We experience fear such as every real knower must undergo; a feeling for the greatness of the Cosmic Spirit who pervades the world. We are in the presence of this greatness and we feel our own powerlessness. We feel also what we might have become in the course of the earth's history, or in that of the Cosmos. We feel our own impotent existence so far removed from Divine existence. We feel fear in face of the ideal we must come to resemble, and of the magnitude of the effort which should lead us to that ideal. As through esotericism we must feel the whole magnitude of the effort, so must we feel this fear as a struggle we take upon ourselves, a wrestling with the Spirit of the Cosmos. When we feel our own little-ness, and the necessary struggle laid upon us to attain our ideal, to become one with that which works and weaves in the world—when we experience this with fear, then only may we lay fear aside and betake ourselves to the path, to the paths which lead us to our ideal. And if we feel this completely and rightly, there comes before us yet another significant Imagination. If we had never read a Gospel, if mankind had never had such an external book, a spiritual picture would rise before our clairvoyant sight.

We are led out into the solitude which stands clearly before the inner eye, and we are brought before the picture of the Ideal Man who in a human body experienced all the im-measurable fears and anguish that we ourselves can taste in this moment. The picture of Christ in Gethsemane stands before us, as He experienced fear to an overwhelmingly intensified degree, the fear that we ourselves must feel on the path of Initiation, the fear that wrung from His brow the Bloody Sweat. That is the picture we encounter at a certain point on our occult path, independently of all external documents. So we have, standing before us like two great pillars on the occult path, the story of the Temptation experienced spiritually, and the scene on the Mount of Olives experienced spiritually. And then we understand the words: Watch and pray, and live in prayer, so that you will never be tempted to remain standing at any one point, but will continually stride forward.

This means that first of all we experience the Gospel; we experience everything so that we could write it down just as the writers of the Gospels have described it. For we do not need to take these two pictures from the Gospel; we can take them out of our own inner consciousness; we can bring them forth out of the Holy of Holies of the soul. No teacher is needed to come and say: 'You must place before yourself in imagination the Temptation, and the scene on the Mount of Olives.' We need only bring before ourselves that which can be developed in our consciousness through meditation, purification of our common human feelings, and so on. Then, without constraint from anyone, we call forth the Imaginations which are contained in the Gospels.

In the Jesuit spiritual movement the pupil had the Gospels given to him first, and afterwards he experienced what the Gospels describe. The way we have indicated to-day shows that when a man has taken the path of the spiritual life, he experiences occultly that which is connected with his own life, and thereby can experience through himself the pictures, the Imaginations, of the Gospels.

LECTURE III

We must now turn our attention to the relation between ordinary religious consciousness and the knowledge that can be gained through higher clairvoyant powers concerning the higher worlds in general, and in particular—this is specially relevant to our theme—concerning the relation of Christ Jesus to these higher worlds.

It will be clear to you all that the evolution of Christianity so far has been such that most persons have not been able to attain through their own clairvoyant knowledge to the mysteries of the Christ-Event. It must be granted that Christianity has entered into the hearts of countless human beings, and to a certain degree its essential nature has been recognised by countless souls; but these hearts and souls have not been able to look up to the higher worlds and so to receive clairvoyant vision of what really took place in human evolution through the Mystery of Golgotha and everything connected with it. Hence the knowledge that can be gained through clairvoyant consciousness itself, or through a person having accepted on one or other ground the communications of the seer concerning the mysteries of Christianity, must be carefully distinguished from the religious inclination to Christ and the intellectual leanings towards Him of a person who knows nothing of clairvoyant investigation.

Now you will all agree that during the centuries since the Mystery of Golgotha there have been men of all degrees of intellectual culture who have accepted the mysteries of Christianity in a deep inner way, and from what has been said lately in various lectures you will have felt that this is quite natural, for—as has been emphasised again and again—it is only in the twentieth century that a renewal of the Christ-Event will take place, for this is when a certain general heightening of human powers of cognition begins. It brings with it the possibility that in the course of the next 3,000 years, and without special clairvoyant preparation, more and more persons will be able to attain a direct vision of Christ Jesus.

This has never happened before. Until now there have been only two—or later on to-day we may perhaps discover three—sources of knowledge concerning the Christian mysteries for persons who could not rise by training to clairvoyant observation. One source was the Gospels and all that comes from the communications in the Gospels, or in the traditions connected with them. The second source of knowledge arose because there have always been clairvoyant individuals who could see into the higher worlds, and through their own knowledge brought down the facts of the Christ-Event. Other persons followed these individuals, receiving from them a 'never-ending Gospel', which could continually come into the world through those who were clairvoyant. These two seem at first to be the only two sources in the evolution of Christian humanity up to the present time. And, now from the twentieth century onwards, a third begins. It arises because for more and more people an extension, an enhancement, of their cognitional powers, not brought about through meditation, concentration and other exercises, will occur. As we have often said, more and more persons will be able to renew for themselves the experience of Paul on the road to Damascus. Hence we can say of the ensuing period that it will provide a direct means of perceiving the significance and the Being of Christ Jesus.

Now the first question that will naturally occur to you is this: What is the essential difference between the clairvoyant vision of Christ which has always been possible as a result of the esoteric development described yesterday, and the vision of Christ which will come to people, without esoteric development, in the next 3,000 years, beginning from our twentieth century?

There is certainly an important difference. And it would be false to believe that what the seer through his clairvoyant development sees to-day in the higher worlds concerning the Christ-Event, and what has been seen clairvoyantly concerning the Christ-Event since the Mystery of Golgotha, is exactly the same as the vision which will come to an ever greater and greater number of people. These are two quite different things. As to how far they differ, we must ask clairvoyant research how it is that from the twentieth century onwards Christ Jesus will enter more and more into the ordinary consciousness of men. The reason is as follows.

Just as on the physical plane in Palestine, at the beginning of our era, an event occurred in which the most important part was taken by Christ Himself—an event which has its significance for the whole of humanity—so in the course of the twentieth century, towards the end of the twentieth century, a significant event will again take place, not in the physical world, but in the world we usually call the world of the etheric. And this event will have as fundamental a significance for the evolution of humanity as the event of Palestine had at the beginning of our era. Just as we must say that for Christ Himself the event of Golgotha had a significance that with this very event a God died, a God overcame death—we will speak later concerning the way this is to be understood; the deed had not happened before and it is an accomplished fact which will not happen again—so an event of profound significance will take place in the etheric world. And the occurrence of this event, an event connected with the Christ Himself, will make it possible for men to learn to see the Christ, to look upon Him.

What is this event? It consists in the fact that a certain office in the Cosmos, connected with the evolution of humanity in the twentieth century, passes over in a heightened form to the Christ. Occult clairvoyant research

tells us that in our epoch Christ becomes the Lord of
Karma for human evolution. This event marks the beginning
of something that we find intimated also in the New
Testament: He will come again to separate, or to bring
about the crisis for, the living and the dead.* Only, according
to occult research, this is not to be understood as though it
were a single event for all time which takes place on the
physical plane. It is connected with the whole future evolution of humanity. And whereas Christianity and Christian
evolution were hitherto a kind of preparation, we now have
the significant fact that Christ becomes the Lord of Karma,
so that in the future it will rest with Him to decide what
our karmic account is, how our credit and debit in life are
related.

This has been common knowledge in Western occultism
for many centuries, and is denied by no occultist who knows
these things. But recently it has been verified again with the
utmost care, by every means available to occult research. We
will now enter more exactly into these matters.

Ask all those who know something of the truth about these
things, and you will find everywhere one fact confirmed, but
a fact which only at this present stage in the development
of our Movement could be made known. Everything
which can make our minds receptive towards such a fact
had first to be gathered together. You can find in occult
literature information concerning these matters if you wish to
search for it. However, I shall take no account of the literature; I shall only bring forward the corresponding facts.

When certain conditions are described, including those I
have dealt with myself, a picture has to be given of the world
a man enters on passing through the gate of death. Now there
are a great many men, especially those who have gone
through the development of Western civilisation—these

* Acts X: 42—To testify that He is the one ordained by God to be
Judge of the living and dead. II Timothy IV:1 —Christ Jesus who is to
judge the living and the dead.

things are not the same for all peoples—who experience a quite definite event in the moment following the separation of the etheric body after death. We know that on passing through the gate of death we separate ourselves from the physical body. The individual is at first still connected for a time with his etheric body, but afterwards he separates his astral body and also his Ego from the etheric body. We know that he takes with him an extract of his etheric body; we know also that the main part of the etheric body goes another way; generally it becomes part of the cosmic ether, either dissolving completely—this happens only under imperfect conditions—or continuing to work on as an enduring active form. When the individual has stripped off his etheric body he passes over into the Kamaloka region for the period of purification in the soul-world. Before this, however, he undergoes a quite special experience which has not previously been mentioned, because, as I said, the time was not ripe for it. Now, however, these things will be fully accepted by all who are qualified to judge them.

Before entering Kamaloka, the individual experiences a meeting with a quite definite Being who presents him with his karmic account. And this Being, who stood there as a kind of bookkeeper for the karmic Powers, had for many men the form of Moses. Hence the mediaeval formula which originated in Rosicrucianism: Moses presents man in the hour of death—the phrase is not quite accurate, but that is immaterial here—Moses presents man in the hour of his death with the record of his sins, and at the same time points to the 'stern law'. Thus the man can recognise how he has departed from this stern law which he ought to have followed.

In the course of our time—and this is the significant point—this office passes over to Christ Jesus, and man will ever more and more meet Christ Jesus as his Judge, his karmic Judge. That is the supersensible event. Just as on the physical plane, at the beginning of our era, the event of Palestine took place, so in our time the office of Karmic

Judge passes over to Christ Jesus in the higher world next to our own. This event works into the physical world, on the physical plane, in such a way that men will develop towards it the feeling that by all their actions they will be causing something for which they will be accountable to the judgment of Christ. This feeling, now appearing quite naturally in the course of human development, will be transformed so that it permeates the soul with a light which little by little will shine out from the individual himself, and will illuminate the form of Christ in the etheric world. And the more this feeling is developed—a feeling that will have stronger significance than the abstract conscience—the more will the etheric Form of Christ be visible in the coming centuries. We shall have to characterise this fact more exactly in the next few days, and we shall then see that a quite new event has come to pass, an event which works into the Christ-development of humanity.

With regard to the evolution of Christianity on the physical plane, let us now ask whether for the non-clairvoyant consciousness there was not also a third way, over against the two already given. Such a third way was in fact always there, for all Christian evolution. It had to be there. The objective evolution of humanity is not directed in accordance with the opinions of men, but in accordance with objective facts.

Concerning Christ Jesus there have been many opinions in the course of the centuries, or the Councils and Church assemblies and theologians would not have disputed so much among themselves; and in no period, perhaps, have so many people held various views of the Christ as in our own. Facts, however, are not determined by human opinions, but by the forces actually present in human evolution. These facts could be recognised by many more people simply through noticing what the Gospels have to say, if people had the patience and perseverance to look at things really without prejudice, and if they were not too quick and biased

in considering the objective facts. Most people, however, do
not want to form a picture of Christ according to the facts,
but one that suits their own likings and represents their own
ideal. And it must be said that in a certain respect Theosophists of all shades of opinion do this very thing to-day.
When, for example, certain highly developed individuals
who have attained an advanced stage of human evolution
are spoken of in theosophical literature as Masters, or Adepts,
this is a truth that cannot be disputed by anyone who knows
the facts. It applies to individuals who have had many
incarnations; through exercises and holy life they have
pressed on in advance of mankind and have acquired powers
which the rest of humanity will acquire only in the future.
It is natural and right that a student of Theosophy who has
acquired some knowledge concerning the Masters, the
Adepts, should feel the highest respect for such lofty individuals. If we go on to contemplate so sublime a life as that
of Buddha, we must agree that Buddha should be looked on
as one of the highest Adepts. And we shall then be able to
gain through our minds and feelings an inward relationship
to such a person.

Now because the Theosophist approaches the figure of
Christ Jesus on the ground of this theosophical knowledge
and feeling, he will naturally feel a certain need—and a very
comprehensible need—to connect with his Christ Jesus the
same concept he has formed of a Master, of an Adept,
perhaps of Buddha; and he may be impelled to say: 'Jesus
of Nazareth must be thought of as a great Adept!' This preconceived opinion would turn upside down any knowledge
of the real nature of Christ. And it would be no more than a
preconceived opinion only prejudice, although an understandable one. How shall someone who has won the deepest,
most intimate relationship to the Christ not place the bearer
of the Christ-Being in the same rank as the Master, the
Adept, or the Buddha? Why should he not? This must
seem to us quite comprehensible. Perhaps to such a person

it would seem like a depreciation of Jesus of Nazareth if we were not to do so. But by applying this concept to Jesus of Nazareth we are led away from directing our thought according to the facts, at least as these facts have found their way to us through tradition. Anyone who examines without bias the traditional records—disregarding all opinions offered by Church Councils and Fathers and so on—will not fail to recognise one fact: Jesus of Nazareth cannot be called an Adept.

Where in tradition do we find anything which allows us to apply to Jesus of Nazareth the concept of the Adept as we have it in theosophical teaching? In the first periods of Christianity one thing was emphasised: that Jesus of Nazareth was a man like any other, a weak man like any other. And those who uphold the saying, 'Jesus was truly man' understand most nearly who it was that came into the world. Thus if we pay proper heed to the tradition, no idea of 'Adept' is to be found there. And if you remember all that has been said in past lectures concerning the development of Jesus of Nazareth—the history of the Jesus-child in whom up to his twelfth year Zarathustra lived, and the history of the other Jesus-child in whom Zarathustra then lived up to his thirtieth year—you will certainly say: Here we have to do with a special man, a man for whose existence the world's history, the world's evolution, made the greatest preparations, evident from the fact that two human bodies were formed, and in one of them up to the twelfth year, and in the other from the twelfth to the thirtieth year, the Zarathustra-individuality dwelt.

Since these two Jesus-figures were such significant individualities, Jesus of Nazareth certainly stands high; but not in the same way as an Adept does, for the Adept goes forward continuously from incarnation to incarnation. And apart from this: in the thirtieth year, when the Christ-Individuality enters into the body of Jesus of Nazareth, this very Jesus of Nazareth forsakes his body, and from the moment of the Baptism by John—even if we do not now speak of the Christ—we have to do with a human being who must be designated in the truest sense of the word as a 'mere man', save that he is the bearer of the Christ. But we must distinguish between the bearer of the Christ and the Christ Himself. Once the body which was to be the bearer of the Christ had been forsaken by the Zarathustra-individuality, there dwelt in it no human individuality who had attained any specially high development. The stage of development shown by Jesus of Nazareth sprang from the fact that the Zarathustra-individuality dwelt in him. As we know, however, this human nature was forsaken by the Zarathustra-individuality. Thus it was that this human nature, directly the Christ-Individuality had taken possession of it, brought against Him all that otherwise comes forth from human nature—the Tempter. That is why the Christ could go through the extremities of despair and sorrow, as shown to us in the happenings on the Mount of Olives.

Anyone who leaves out of account these essential points cannot come to a real knowledge of the Being of the Christ. The Christ-bearer was truly man—not an Adept. Recognition of this fact will open for us a first glimpse into the whole nature of the events of Golgotha, the events of Palestine. If we were to look upon Christ Jesus simply as a high Adept, we should have to place Him in a line with other Adept-natures. Some people may perhaps tell us that we do not do this because from the very outset, owing to some preconceived idea, we want to place Christ Jesus beyond all other Adepts, as a still higher Adept. Those who might say this are not aware of what we have to impart as the results of occult research in our time.

The question is not in the very least whether the prestige of other Adepts would be impaired. Within the world-conception to which we must adhere according to the occult results of the present time, we know just as well as others that there existed as a contemporary of Christ Jesus another

significant individuality whom we regard as a true Adept.
And unless we go into exact details, it is even difficult for us
to distinguish inwardly this human being from Christ Jesus,
for he really appears quite like Him. When, for instance, we
hear that this contemporary of Christ Jesus was announced
before his birth by a heavenly vision, it reminds us of the
annunciation of the birth of Jesus, as told in the Gospels.
When we hear that he was not designated merely as of
human birth, but as a son of the Gods, this reminds us again
of the beginning of the Gospels of Matthew and Luke. When
we hear that the birth of this individuality took his mother
by surprise, so that she was overwhelmed, we are reminded
of the birth of Jesus of Nazareth, and of the events in Bethle-
hem, as told in the Gospels. When we hear that the individuality grew up and surprised all around him by his wise
answers to the questions from the priests, it reminds us of the
scene of the twelve-year-old Jesus in the Temple. When we
are told that this individuality came to Rome and met there
the funeral procession of a young girl, that the procession
was brought to a halt and that he awakened the dead, we
are reminded of an awakening from the dead in the Gospel
of Luke. And if we wish to speak of miracles, numberless
miracles are recorded in connection with this individuality,
who was a contemporary of Christ Jesus. Indeed, the simi-
larity goes so far that after the death of this individuality
he is said to have appeared to men, as Christ Jesus appeared after His death to the disciples. And when from
the Christian side all possible reasons are brought forward
either to depreciate this being or to deny altogether
his historical existence, this is no less ingenious than what is
said against the historical existence of Christ Jesus Himself.
The individuality in question is Apollonius of Tyana, and of
him we speak as a really high Adept.

If we now ask about the essential difference between
the Christ Jesus event and the Apollonius event, we must be
clear what the important point in the Apollonius event is.

Apollonius of Tyana is an individuality who went through many incarnations; he won for himself high powers and reached a certain climax in his incarnation at the beginning of our era. Hence the individual we are considering is he who lived in the body of Apollonius of Tyana and had therein his earthly field of action. It is with him that we are concerned. Now we know that a human individuality takes part in the building up of his earthly body. Hence we must say: the body of this individuality was built up by him to a certain form for his own particular use. This we cannot say of Christ Jesus. In the thirtieth year of Jesus of Nazareth the Christ came into the physical body, etheric body and astral body of Jesus; hence He had not himself built up this body from childhood. The relationship between the Christ-Individuality and this body is quite different from that between the Apollonius-individuality and his body. When in the spirit we turn our gaze to Apollonius of Tyana, we say: 'It is the concern of this individuality, and his concern plays itself out as the life of Apollonius of Tyana.' If we want to represent in a diagram a life-course of this kind, we can do it like this:

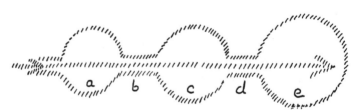

Let the continuous individuality be shown by the horizontal line; then we have in (a) a first incarnation, in (b) a life between death and a new birth, in (c) a second incarnation followed again by (d) a life between death and a new birth, then a third incarnation, (e) and so on. That which passes through all these incarnations—the human individuality— is like a thread of human life, independent of the sheaths of the astral body, etheric body and physical body, and also, between death and a new birth, independent of those parts of the etheric body and astral body which remain behind. Thus the life-thread is always separated from the external Cosmos.

If we want to represent the nature of the Christ-life, we must draw it otherwise. When we consider the preceding incarnations of Jesus of Nazareth, the Christ-life certainly develops in a certain way. But when we draw the life-thread, we have to show that in the thirtieth year of the life of Jesus of Nazareth the individuality forsakes this body, so that from now onwards we have only the sheaths of physical body, etheric body and astral body.

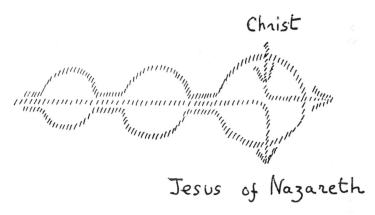

The forces which the individuality develops, however, are not in the external sheaths. They lie in the life-thread of the Ego, which goes from incarnation to incarnation. Thus the forces which belonged to the Zarathustra-individuality, and were present in the body of Jesus of Nazareth, preparing that body, pass out with the Zarathustra-individuality. Hence the sheaths which remain are a normal human organism, not in any sense the organism of an Adept, but the organism of a simple man, a weak man. And now the objective event occurs: whereas in other cases the life-thread simply goes farther, as in (a) and (b), it now turns along a sidepath (c);

for through the Baptism by John in Jordan the Christ-Being entered into the three-fold organism. In this organism the Christ-Being lived from the Baptism until the thirty-third year, until the Event of Golgotha, as we have often described.

Whose concern, then, is the life of Christ Jesus from the thirtieth to the thirty-third year? It is not the concern of the individuality who went from incarnation to incarnation, but of that Individuality who from out of the Cosmos entered into the body of Jesus of Nazareth; the concern of an Individuality, a Being who was never before connected with the earth, who from out of the Universe connected Himself with a human body. In this sense the event which took place between the thirtieth and thirty-third years of the life of Christ Jesus, between the John-Baptism and the Mystery of Golgotha, are those of the Divine Being, Christ, not of a man. Hence this event was not a concern of the earth but a concern of the supersensible worlds, for it had nothing to do with a man. As a sign of this—that it had to do with no man—the human being who had dwelt in this body up to the thirtieth year forsook it.

These happenings have originally something to do with events that took place before such a life-thread as our human one had passed into a physical human organization. We must go back to the ancient Lemurian time, into the age wherein human individualities, coming from Divine heights, incarnated for the first time in earthly bodies; back to the event which is indicated for us in the Old Testament as the Temptation through the Serpent. This event is of a very remarkable kind. From its outcome all men suffer as long as they are subject to incarnation. For if this event had not happened, the whole evolution of mankind on the earth would have been different, and men would have passed in a much more perfect condition from incarnation to incarnation. Through this event, however, they become more closely entangled in matter, allegorically designated as the 'Fall of Man'. But it was the Fall that first called man to his present individuality; so that, as he goes as an individuality from incarnation to incarnation, he is not responsible for the Fall. We know that the Luciferic spirits were responsible for the Fall. Hence we must say that before man became man in the earthly sense, there occurred the divine, super-sensible event by which a deeper entanglement in matter was laid upon him. Through this event man has indeed attained to the power of love and to freedom, but through it something was laid upon him that he could not lay upon himself by his own power. This becoming entangled in matter was not a human act, but a deed of the Gods, which happened before men could co-operate in their own fate. It is something which the Higher Powers of progressive evolution arranged with the Luciferic powers. We shall have to go into all these events and characterise them more exactly. To-day we will place only the chief point before our minds.

What happened at that time needed a counterpoise. The pre-human event—the Fall of Man—needed a counterpoise, but this again was a concern not of human beings, but of the Gods among themselves. And we shall see that this action had to take its course as deeply in matter as the first action had taken place above it. The God had to descend as deeply into matter as He had allowed man to sink into matter.

Let this fact work upon you with its full weight; then you will understand that this incarnation of the Christ in Jesus of Nazareth was something that concerned Christ Himself. And what part was man called upon to take in it? First of all, as spectator, to see how the God compensates for the Fall, how He provides the compensating act. It would not have been possible to do this within the personality of an Adept, for an Adept is one who by his own efforts has worked his way out of the Fall. It was possible only in a personality who was truly man—who, as man, did not surpass other men. This personality had surpassed them before he was thirty years of age—but no longer. Through that which then took place, a Divine event was accomplished in the evolution of mankind, just as had been done at the beginning of human evolution in the Lemurian time. And men were partakers in a transaction which had taken place among Gods; men could look upon it, because the Gods had to make use of the world of the physical plane in order to let their transaction play itself out to the end. Hence it is much better to say: 'Christ offered to the Gods the atonement which He could offer only in a physical human body', than to use any other form of words. Man was a spectator of a Divine occasion.

Through this atonement something had happened for human nature. Men simply experienced it in the course of their development. Thereby the third way was opened, besides the two already indicated.

Men who have gone deeply into the nature of Christianity have often pointed out these three ways. From among the large number of those who could be named I will mention only two who have given eminent testimony to the fact that Christ—who from the twentieth century onwards will be seen through the more highly developed faculties—can be recognised, felt, experienced, through feelings which were not possible in the same form before the Event of Golgotha.

There is, for example, a man who in his whole cast of mind can be looked upon as a sharp opponent of what we have characterised as Jesuitism: Blaise Pascal, a great figure in spiritual history, standing forth as one who has set aside all that had arisen to the detriment of the old Churches, but has also absorbed nothing of modern rationalism. As always with great minds, he really remained alone with his thoughts. But what is the fundamental feature of his thinking at the beginning of the modern period? When we look into the matter we see from the writings he left behind, particularly from his inspiring *Pensées*—a book accessible to anyone— how he perceived and felt what man must have become if the Christ-Event had not taken place in the world.

In the secrecy of his soul, Pascal set himself the question: What would have become of man if no Christ had entered into human evolution? And he replied: We can feel that in his soul man encounters two dangers. One danger is that he should recognise God as identical with his own being: knowledge of God in knowledge of man. Whither does this lead? When it arises so that man recognises himself as God, it leads to pride, haughtiness, arrogance; and man destroys his best powers because he hardens them in haughtiness and pride. This is a knowledge of God that would always have been possible, even if no Christ had come, even if the Christ-Event had not worked as an impulse in the hearts of all men. Human beings would always have been able to recognize God, but they would have become proud through this consciousness in their own breasts. Or there might be human beings who hide themselves from the knowledge of God, who want to know nothing about God. Their gaze falls on something else; it falls on human powerlessness, on human misery, and then of necessity there follows human despair. That would have been the other danger, the danger of those who had put away from them the knowledge of God.

Only these two ways, said Pascal, are possible: pride and arrogance, or despair. Then the Christ-Event entered into human evolution, and worked so that every man received a power which not only enabled him to experience God, but the very God who had become like unto men, who had lived with men. That is the sole remedy for pride: when we turn our gaze upon the God who bowed Himself to the Cross; when the soul looks to Christ bowing Himself to death on the Cross. And that, too, is the only healing for despair. For this is not a humility that makes a man weak, but a humility that gives healing strength which transcends despair. As the mediator between pride and despair, there dawns in the human soul the Helper, the Saviour, as Pascal understood Him. This can be felt by every man, even without clairvoyance. This is the preparation for the Christ who from the twentieth century onwards will be visible for all men; who as the Healer for pride and despair will arise in every human breast, but earlier could not be felt in the same way.

The second witness I would summon from the long line of men who have this feeling, a feeling that every Christian can make his own, is one already mentioned in many other connections, Vladimir Soloviev. Soloviev also points to two powers in human nature, between which the personal Christ must stand as a mediator. There is a duality, he says, for which the human soul longs: immortality, and wisdom or moral perfection; but neither belongs to human nature from the start. Human nature shares the characteristic of all natures, and nature leads not to immortality, but to death. In beautiful meditations this great thinker of modern times works out how external science shows that death extends over everything. If we look at external nature, our knowledge replies, 'Death is!' But within us lives the longing for immortality. Why? Because of our longing for perfection. We have only to glance into the human soul to see that a longing for perfection lives in us. Just as truly, says Soloviev, as the red rose is endowed with red colour, so truly is the human soul endowed with the longing for perfection. But to strive after perfection without longing for immortality, he continues, is to give the lie to existence. It would be meaningless if the soul were to end with death, as all natural being ends. Yet all natural existence tells us, 'Death is!' Hence the human soul is under the necessity of going beyond natural existence and seeking the answer elsewhere.

Proceeding from this thought, Soloviev says: Look at the natural scientists, what answer do they give when they wish to teach the connection of the human soul with nature? A mechanical natural order, they say, prevails and man is part of it. And what do the philosophers answer? That the spiritual, meaning an empty abstract thought-world which pervades all the facts of nature, is to be recognised

philosophically. Neither of these statements is an answer
for a man who is conscious of himself, and asks from out
of his consciousness, 'What is perfection?' If he is conscious
that he has a longing for perfection, a longing for the life
of truth, if he asks what Power can satisfy this longing,
there opens for him an outlook into a realm, the realm of
Grace over and above nature, which at first stands before
the soul as a riddle; and unless the answer to it can be
found, the soul is constrained to regard itself as a falsehood.
No philosophy, no natural science, can connect the realm
of Grace with existence, for natural forces work mechani-
cally, and thought-powers have only thought-reality. But
what is it that is able, with full reality, to unite the soul
with nature? He Who is the personal Christ working in
the world. And only the living Christ, not one that is
merely thought of, can give the answer. Anything that works
merely in the soul leaves the soul alone, for the soul cannot of
itself give birth to the kingdom of Grace. That which
transcends nature, which like nature itself stands there as a
real fact, the personal historic Christ—He it is who gives not
an intellectual answer but a real answer.

And now Soloviev comes to the most complete, the most
fully spiritual answer that can be given at the end of the
period now closing, before the doors open to that which has
so often been intimated to you: the vision of Christ which
will have its beginning in the twentieth century. In the light
of these facts, a name can be given to the consciousness which
Pascal and Soloviev have so memorably described: we can
call it Faith. So, too, it has been named by others.

With the concept of Faith we can come from two directions
into a strange conflict regarding the human soul. Go through
the evolution of the concept of Faith and see what the critics
have said about it. To-day men are so far advanced that they
say Faith must be guided by knowledge, and a Faith not
supported by knowledge must be put aside. Faith must be
dethroned, as it were, and replaced by knowledge. In the

Middle Ages the things of the Higher Worlds were appre-
hended by Faith, and Faith was held to be justified on its
own account.

The fundamental principle of Protestantism, also, is that
Faith, alongside knowledge, is to be looked upon as justified.
Faith is something which goes forth from the human soul,
and alongside of it is the knowledge which ought to be
common to all. It is interesting to see how Kant, whom many
consider a great philosopher, did not get beyond this
concept of Faith. His idea is that what a man should attain
concerning such matters as God, immortality and so forth,
ought to shine in from quite other regions, but only through a
moral faith, not through knowledge.

The highest development of the concept of Faith comes
with Soloviev, who stands before the closed door as the most
significant thinker of his time, pointing already to the
modern world. For Soloviev knows a Faith quite different
from all previous concepts of it. Whither has the prevailing
concept of Faith led humanity? It has brought humanity to
the atheistic, materialistic demand for mere knowledge of
the external world, in line with Lutheran and Kantian ideas,
or in the sense of the Monistic philosophy of the nineteenth
century; to the demand for the knowledge which boasts
of knowledge, and considers Faith as something that the
human soul had framed for itself out of its necessary weakness
up to a certain time in the past. The concept of Faith has
finally come to this, because Faith was regarded as merely
subjective. In the preceding centuries Faith had been de-
manded as a necessity. In the nineteenth century Faith is
attacked just because it finds itself in opposition to the
universally valid knowledge which should stem from the
human soul.

And then comes a philosopher who recognises and prizes
the concept Faith in order to attain a relationship to Christ
that had not previously been possible. He sees this Faith, in so
far as it relates to Christ, as an act of necessity, of inner duty.

For with Soloviev the question is not, 'to believe or not to
believe'; Faith is for him a necessity in itself. His view is that
we have a duty to believe in Christ, for otherwise we paralyse
ourselves and give the lie to our existence. As the crystal form
emerges in a mineral substance, so does Faith arise in the
human soul as something natural to itself. Hence the soul
must say: 'If I recognise the truth, and not a lie about
myself, then in my own soul I must realise Faith. Faith is a
duty laid upon me, but I cannot do otherwise than come to it
through my own free act.' And therein Soloviev sees the
distinctive mark of the Christ-Deed, that Faith is both a
necessity and at the same time a morally free act. It is as
though it were said to the soul: You can do nothing else. If
you do not wish to extinguish the self within you, you must
acquire Faith for yourself; but it must be by your own free
act! And, like Pascal, Soloviev brings that which the soul
experiences, in order not to feel itself a lie, into connection
with the historic Christ Jesus as He entered into human
evolution through the events in Palestine. Because of this,
Soloviev says: If Christ had not entered into human evolution, so that He has to be thought of as the historic Christ;
if He had not brought it about that the soul perceives the
inwardly free act as much as the lawful necessity of Faith,
the human soul in our post-Christian times would feel itself
bound to extinguish itself and to say, not 'I am', but 'I am
not'. That, according to this philosopher, would have been
the course of evolution in post-Christian times: an inner
consciousness would have permeated the human soul with
the 'I am not'.* Directly the soul pulls itself together to the
point of attributing real existence to itself, it cannot do otherwise than turn back to the historic Christ Jesus.

Here we have, for exoteric thought also, a step forward
along the path of Faith in establishing the third way.

* Cf. Carlyle's famous account in Sartor Resartus, Book II, Chapter
VII, of his encounter with a repudiation of the 'Everlasting No'. (Translator's note.)

Through the message of the Gospels, a person not able to look into the spiritual world can come to recognition of Christ. Through that which the consciousness of the seer can impart to him, he can likewise come to a recognition of the Christ. But there was also a third way, the way of self-knowledge, and as the witnesses cited, together with thousands and thousands of other human beings, can testify from their own experience, it leads to a recognition that self-knowledge in post-Christian time is impossible without placing Christ Jesus by the side of man and a corresponding recognition that the soul must either deny itself, or, if it wills to affirm itself, it must at the same time affirm Christ Jesus.

Why this was not so in pre-Christian times will be shown in the next few days.

LECTURE IV

We can perhaps sum up the outcome of the last lecture in the following way. From the Mystery of Golgotha until the coming of the epoch at whose portal we now stand, a man could attain by various exoteric means to an experience of the Christ-Impulse—an experience preceding any actual Initiation. One of these exoteric ways is through the Gospels, through the New Testament. The contents of the Gospels, when they are received into our souls and permitted to work upon us, can in fact bring about for each one of us an inner experience, and this inner experience may indeed be called the Christ-Experience. The second way for the exotericist was described as that of accepting what an esotericist—he who in a certain sense has been initiated—could make known from the spiritual worlds. By this way also the man who as yet was standing before the gate of Initiation could come to the Christ-Event, not through the traditional Gospels, but through continuous revelations from the spiritual worlds.

Yesterday, too, we spoke of a third way, that of the inner deepening of heart and soul, and we pointed out that this way must arise in the soul from feelings; but with the proviso that if a man feels within him only the Divine spark, he may be driven to pride and arrogance. On the other hand, if he is not conscious of his connection with the Divine, he can be driven to despair. We have seen how in fact the swaying between despair on the one hand, and pride and arrogance on the other, if at the same time a man fixes his gaze upon the events in Palestine, can lead on to the birth of the Christ-Event within him.

It was then pointed out that within the next 3,000 years, beginning from our own epoch, everything concerning the evolution of humanity will change. We also indicated the significant event which follows from the Mystery of Golgotha, but will be seen only in the supersensible worlds. We pointed out that the capacities of human beings will be enhanced, and that, from our own epoch onwards, a sufficiently large number of persons will grow up able to look on the Christ. That which has hitherto had a justified place in the world as Faith will be replaced by what may be called the Vision of Christ.

Now it will be our task to show further how from the usual way of experiencing Christ, as an experience of the heart, the path opens out quite naturally to what may be called the Christian Initiation. In the next few days we shall speak more exactly about the gradual building up of the Christian Initiation and we shall also need to characterise more closely the nature of the Christ-Event. Thus a picture of the Christian-Initiation, and of the Christ-Event, from the Baptism by John to the consummation of the Mystery of Golgotha, should come before our souls.

If you keep this summary in mind, the following quite justified question may arise. What is the relation between external Christianity, Christian evolution, as it appears in world history, and the Christ-Event itself? To everyone who stands consciously in the present, who has gone through no special soul-experience of a mystical kind, or has perhaps the preliminary stages of esotericism behind him, it must appear strange that in every human being a quite definite kind of soul-experience should be so dependent upon an historic fact—the events in Palestine, on Golgotha—and that previously for these human souls something was not possible which afterwards, through these events, became possible, namely the inner Christ-Experience.

The leaders of the first Christians, and also the first Christians generally, had a very distinct consciousness of these facts, and in preparation for the coming days it will be well to consider a little how these things appeared to their minds.

One can easily believe—and later this belief turned more and more into an orthodox, very one-sided view—that human beings of the pre-Christian times were radically different from those of the post-Christian period. That this view is one-sided you can gather from the words of Augustine: 'What we now call the Christian religion existed already among the ancients, and was not lacking in the earliest days of the human race. When Christ appeared in the flesh, the true religion, which was already in existence, received the name of Christianity.' In the days of Augustine it was well known that there was not so radical a difference between pre-Christian and post-Christian times as orthodoxy maintained.

Justin Martyr, too, makes a quite remarkable statement in his writings. Justin, who is recognised by the Church as one of the Fathers and a martyr, enlarges upon the relation of Socrates and Heraclitus to Christ. With a certain simple clarity he sees in Christ that which we set forth yesterday in the relation of Christ to Jesus of Nazareth, and he works out his idea of the Christ Being accordingly. In his *Apologia* he says, in the context of his own time, something we can repeat to-day in the same words: Christ, or the Logos, was incarnated in the man, Jesus of Nazareth. Justin then asks: Was the Logos not present in eminent personalities of pre-Christian times? Was man in pre-Christian times quite unacquainted with the Logos? To this question Justin Martyr answers No. Socrates and Heraclitus were also men in whom the Logos lived. They did not possess the Logos completely; but through the Christ-Event it became possible for a man to experience inwardly the Logos in its complete original form.

From such a passage by a recognised Father of the Church we can gather, first, that the early Christians were acquainted with something which, after having been, as Augustine says, 'always there', had entered into the evolution of the earth in an enhanced form through the Mystery of Golgotha.

Secondly, we have an answer from the earliest Christian centuries to the question we ourselves have raised to-day. Men such as Justin Martyr were still near to the Event of Golgotha, and they knew much more than we can about the nature of those who were but a few centuries removed from them, as Heraclitus and Socrates were. Justin held that in the time of Socrates, although such an eminent man could experience the Logos within himself, he could not experience it fully in its most intense form. And that is important. As testimony from those early times it indicates— if we look away from the event of Golgotha—how it was felt that between the centuries before and after Christ there was something whereby pre-Christian men could be distinguished from post-Christian. It can be shown from numerous other historical instances that men in earlier centuries consciously said, 'Human nature has indeed changed; it has acquired another quality.' Someone living in the third century after Christ, looking back to men who had lived in the third century before Christ, could say that although in their own way they could penetrate deeply into the secrets of existence, yet something that could happen in men living after the time of Christ could not have happened previously. The message of John the Baptist, 'Change your outlook on the world, your idea of the world, for the times have become other than they were'—a statement confirmed by occult science—continued to be strongly and intensely felt.

It must be grasped quite clearly that if we want to understand human evolution, we must give up the false idea that man has always been as he is to-day. For—apart from the fact that in the West no meaning could then be attached to the idea of reincarnation—tradition and occult science are at one in showing that in early times human beings really possessed something which now exists only in the subconscious, namely a certain power of clairvoyance; that later they descended from this height of clairvoyance, and that the lowest point in this descending evolution, when those forces developed which obscured the old clairvoyant powers, lies in the time of the Mystery of Golgotha.

We know that in the material sphere a great quantity of fluid can be affected by the infusion of a very small quantity of a given substance. If you put a drop of some substance into a suitable fluid, it spreads through the fluid and colours the whole of it. In the material sphere, everyone understands this. But it is impossible to understand spiritual life if this principle is not understood in a spiritual sense. Our earth is not merely the material body we see with our eyes; it has a spiritual sheath. As we ourselves have an etheric body and an astral body, so the earth has such higher bodies. And just as a small quantity of substance spreads through a fluid, so that which rayed forth spiritually from the Act on Golgotha spread through the spiritual atmosphere of the earth, permeated it, and is still there. Something new has thus been imparted to our earth. And since souls do not merely live everywhere enclosed by matter, but are like drops in the sea of the earthly-spiritual, even so are human beings embedded in the spiritual atmosphere of our earth, which is permeated by the Christ-Impulse. That was not so before the Mystery of Golgotha, and it marks the great difference between pre-Christian and post-Christian life. If a person cannot imagine such a thing happening in spiritual life, he is not yet far enough advanced to grasp Christianity truly as a mystical fact, the full meaning of which can be recognised and acknowledged only in the spiritual world.

Anyone who looks back over the unedifying disputes concerning the being and personality of Jesus of Nazareth, and the Being and Individuality of the Christ, will be able to feel everywhere in the gnostic and mystical views of the early Christian centuries that the most advanced of those who were concerned to extend Christianity stood with reverent awe before this mystical fact. Even though the words and phrases of Christian teachers are often abstruse, we can see clearly that these teachers stand in reverent awe before all that came

to pass for the world's evolution through Christianity. Again
and again they declare that weak human understanding, and
the feeble powers of human feeling and perception, are
inadequate to express truly the immense significance and
depth of all that happened through the Mystery of Golgotha.
A powerlessness to give real expression to the highest
truths that man has to grope for—this is something that
passes like a magic breath through the first Christian
teachings. The reading of such writings is a good lesson for
anyone, even in our times. We can learn thereby to exercise a
certain modesty with regard to the highest truths. If we have
the necessary humility and modesty towards things that are
more easily recognised at the portal of a new Christian epoch
than they were in the first Christian centuries, we can say:
Certainly it is now possible to know more than could be
known then, but no one who ventures to speak of the
mysteries of Christianity should remain unconscious of the
fact that what we are able to say to-day concerning the
deepest truths of human evolution will in a comparatively
short time be imperfect again. And because we wish to come
gradually to a deeper characterisation of Christianity, we
must pay special attention at this juncture to a person's
inward attitude towards the spiritual world, if he accepts or
wishes to spread abroad the truths which since the nineteenth
and the beginning of the twentieth century can stream into
us.

Thus, even if we do not speak much about the concept of
Grace, we must make great use of it in practice. Every
occultist today clearly understands that this concept of Grace
must belong to his inner practice of life in a quite special
degree. What does this mean?

It means that to-day investigations can be made concerning the deepest truths of Christianity, quite independently
of the Gospels and of every tradition. Everything, however,
which is connected with a certain thirst for knowledge, with a
passion for gaining as quickly as possible a certain number of

ideas, will lead, if not into complete error, quite certainly to
a distortion of the truth. Anyone who says that since he is
occultly prepared, he must provide an explanation, for
example of the Pauline Epistles or the Gospel of Matthew,
showing how their content is to be understood—anyone who
set out to do that and believed he could complete it within
a fixed time would quite certainly deceive himself. In a
human way we can go deeply into these documents, but all
that can be known about them cannot be made known to-day.
For there is a golden saying which applies precisely to the
occult investigator: 'Have patience and wait, until you no
longer wish to grasp the fruits by your own efforts, but they
come to you.'

Many a person can approach the Pauline Epistles feeling
himself ready to understand this or that, because in the
spiritual world it meets his opened eyes. Should he wish at
the same time to understand another passage, perhaps quite
close to it, he may not be able to do so. A curbing of this thirst
for knowledge is necessary to-day. One should rather say to
oneself: 'Grace has brought me to a certain number of
truths. I will wait patiently until further truths flow to me.'
To-day there is really more need for a certain passive attitude
towards these truths than there was perhaps twenty years
ago. This attitude is necessary because our minds must first
completely ripen in order to allow truths to enter into us in
their right form. This is a practical lesson regarding investigation of the spiritual worlds, especially in their relation to
the Christ-Event. It is fundamentally wrong when people
think they can grasp at that which ought to stream towards
them in a certain passive way. For we must be conscious that
we can be what we ought to be only in so far as we are
judged worthy by the spiritual Powers to be this or that. And
all that we can do by way of meditation, contemplation, and
so forth, is really done only to open our eyes, not in order to
seize the truths, but to let them come to us, for we may not
run after them.

Those who through this inward passivity have developed feelings of whole-hearted devotion in the sense described—and with no other feelings can one enter the spiritual world—are ready to understand the fact we have placed in the forefront of our subject to-day: the fact that something like a drop of spiritual substance flowed from the Deed on Golgotha. In our time souls are ripe for this understanding. If it were not so we would have lacked many things that our modern period has brought forth. I need mention only one example: if the soul of Richard Wagner had not ripened in a certain passive way, if concerning the Mystery of Golgotha he had not in some sense surmised the flowing forth of that which came drop by drop into the spiritual atmosphere of earthly humanity, we could not have had his Parsifal. We can discern this in the passages where he refers to the significance of the Blood of Christ. In our day we can find many such minds which show how the spiritual substance which hovers in the atmosphere is grasped by the souls into which it penetrates.

Spiritual Science is here because many more souls now have the possibility of being able, without realising it, to gather from the spiritual world the influences described above; but they need to have their difficulties lightened by an understanding of the spiritual world. In fact, no one whose heart is unripe enters into Spiritual Science; no one who has not more or less of a sincere longing to know something of what has just been mentioned. It may indeed be that some are impelled into our Movement by curiosity or the like, but those who come in with upright hearts feel the longing to be able to open their souls towards that which is making ready for the future epoch of human evolution which begins in our time. People need Spiritual Science to-day because their souls are becoming different from what they were a short time ago. Just as souls underwent a great change during the period in which the Event of Golgotha fell, so will they again experience a great change in this millennium and in the

succeeding ones. The rise of our Movement is connected
with the fact that souls, even if they are not clearly conscious
of it, have an obscure feeling that something of the kind is
going on in our time.

For this reason it became necessary, on the ground of
anthroposophical development, that a certain explanation of
the foundations of the Gospels should be begun. And if you
can convince yourselves through honest inner feeling that
there is something true in the Christ Event, as it was described
in the last lecture, you will find you can understand what
has happened as regarding the explanation of the Gospels.
You will understand that the anthroposophical interpretation
of the Gospels differs radically from all previous interpretations. Anyone who takes up our printed lecture-cycles on
the Gospels, or recalls them from memory, will see that
everywhere a return has been made to true meanings, which
can no longer be found simply by reading the present-day
Gospel texts. From the existing translations, in fact, we can
no longer reach that which the Gospels wish to indicate. To a
certain extent, as they exist to-day, they are no longer fully
of use. What, then, has been done towards reaching an
explanation of the Christ event, and what must be done?

To those who approach an understanding of the Christ-
Event by the path of Spiritual Science, it must be clear that
these Gospels were written by men who could look upon the
Christ-Event spiritually with spiritual eyes. Hence they had
no wish to write an external biography, but followed the old
Initiation writings. (This connection is shown in greater
detail in my book, *Christianity as Mystical Fact.*) They maintained that what had taken place in the depths of the
Mysteries had, in the Christ-Event, occurred on the plane of
history through the divine ordering of human evolution.
What had happened on a small scale within the Mysteries
to the candidates for Initiation was carried out by the Being
we call the Christ on the great stage of world history,
without the preparation that was necessary for human

beings, and without the seclusion of the Mysteries. That which had previously been seen only by the pupil of the Mysteries, in their innermost sanctuary, was enacted before all eyes. This again is something for which the first Christian teachers felt a reverential awe. When they considered what the Gospels ought to be, there arose in the genuine Christian teachers a feeling of their own unworthiness, of their inability to grasp the true kernel and meaning of the Gospels.

This fact is the cause of something else connected with the necessity of interpreting the Gospels as we do to-day in our Movement. If you have followed the explanations of the Gospels given here, you will have noticed that the traditional books of the Gospels are not, in the first place, taken as the basis, for what they say is regarded as something altogether unreliable. Instead, through the reading of the Akashic record, we are taken back to the spiritual writing as it is given out by those who can themselves read spiritually. Only when explanatory reference is made to some passage do we take into account the sentence as it stands in the printed books. We then examine whether, or how far, it agrees with the form that can be recovered from the Akashic record. The Gospels of Matthew, Mark and Luke must be reconstructed in this way from the Akashic record. Only a comparison of the tradition with the original form can show how this or that passage must be read. Every tradition which rests only upon the printed text is bound to go astray and to fall into error. In the future the Gospels must be not only explained, but first reconstructed in their true original form. Then, when anyone examines what is there set forth, he will no longer be able to say that this may or may not be true, for where agreement is shown it will be clear why for us it is only the reading in the Akashic record which can guarantee the right text of the Gospels. And then the Gospels will again be evidence for the correctness of what stands written there. This can be shown in numberless passages. As an example let us take the following:

When at the condemnation of Christ Jesus He was asked whether He was a king sent from God, He replied: 'Thou sayest it!' Now anyone who thinks straightforwardly, and does not wish to explain the Gospels according to the professorial methods of the present day, must admit that with this answer of Christ Jesus no clear sense can be connected in terms either of feeling or of reason. From the side of feeling, we must ask why Christ Jesus speaks so indefinitely that no one can recognise what He means by saying 'Thou sayest it'. If He means 'Thou art right', there is no meaning in it, for the words of the interrogator are not a declaration but a question. How then can this be an answer full of meaning? Or, from the side of reason, how can we think that He whom we imagine to be possessed of all-comprehending wisdom should choose such a form for His answer? When, however, these words are given as they stand in the Akashic record, they have quite another sense. For in the Akashic record it is not 'Thou sayest it', but, 'This, thou alone mayest give as answer', which means, when we understand it rightly, 'To thy question I should have to give an answer that no one may ever give with reference to himself: it can be given only by someone who stands opposite him. Whether the answer is true or not true, of that I cannot speak; the acknowledgement of this truth lies not with me but with thee. Thou must say it; then and then only would it have a meaning.'

Now you may say: 'That may be true or may not be true.' As an abstract judgment that would certainly be correct. But if we look at the whole scene and ask ourselves, 'Can we understand it better when we take the version from the Akashic record?', it will be apparent to everyone that this scene can be understood only in this way. We can say, too, that the last transcriber or translator of this passage did not understand it, because of its difficulty, and so wrote down something inaccurate. Anyone who knows how many things in the world are inexactly written down will not be surprised that here we have to do with an inaccurate version. Have we then no right, when a new epoch of humanity is beginning, to lead the Gospels back to their original form, which can be authenticated from the Akashic record? The whole thing comes out clearly—and this can be shown even from external history—if we consider in this connection the Matthew Gospel. The best that has been said about the origin of the Matthew Gospel may be read in the third volume of Blavatsky's *Secret Doctrine*, a work which must be understood if we are to judge and value it correctly.

There was a certain Father of the Church, Jerome, who wrote towards the end of the fourth century. From what he writes we learn something that can be fully confirmed by occult research: the Gospel of Matthew was originally written in Hebrew. In the copy that Jerome had obtained, or, as we should perhaps say nowadays, in the edition he possessed, he had before him the original language of this Gospel, written in the Hebrew letters still in use, though its language was not the customary Hebrew of that time. Jerome's Bishop had given him the task of translating this version of the Matthew Gospel for his Christians. As a translator Jerome behaved in a most singular way. In the first place he thought it would be dangerous to translate this Gospel of Matthew as it was, because there were things in it which those who up to then had possessed it as their sacred writing wished to keep from the profane world. He thought that this Gospel, if it were translated complete, would cause disturbance rather than edification. So he omitted the things which, according to his own and the ecclesiastical views of that period, might have a disturbing effect, and replaced them by others. But we can learn still more from his writings, and this is the most serious aspect of the whole proceeding: Jerome knew that the Gospel of Matthew could be understood only by those who were initiated into certain secrets. He knew, too, that he was not one of those. In other words, he admitted that he did not understand this Gospel! Yet he translated it. Thus the Matthew Gospel lies before us to-day in the dress given to it by a man who did not understand it, but who became so accustomed to this version that he afterwards condemned as heresy anything asserted about this Gospel if it was not in accord with his own rendering. These are absolute facts.

The next point of interest we must examine is the following. Why, in the very earliest days of Christianity, did those who held specially to the Gospel of Matthew communicate it only to such persons as were initiated into the secret meaning of certain things?

It is possible to understand why this was so only if we are somewhat familiar with the character of Initiation. Such things have often been spoken of to you in one connection or another, and in particular you have heard that Initiation, when by means of it a man attains clairvoyant power, leads him to acquire knowledge of certain fundamental truths concerning the world. These fundamental truths are such that to the ordinary consciousness they at first appear absurd. All it can say about them is: That is a paradox. But there is more to it than that. If the highest truths, i.e. those accessible to an Initiate, were to become known to an unprepared individual—either if he were to conjecture them, which in a certain case might be possible, or if they were imparted to him when he was in an imperfect condition to receive them— then, even if they were the most elementary truths, they would be in the highest degree dangerous for him. Even if the purest, the highest, truth concerning the world were set before him, it would work destructively on him and on his surroundings.

For this reason, anyone to-day who is in possession of the highest truths knows that it cannot be right merely to call someone to him and impart to him the highest mysteries of the world. The highest truths cannot be so imparted that a mouth simply pronounces them and an ear simply hears them. The way in which the highest truths are imparted is quite different. A person who wishes to become a pupil is slowly and gradually prepared, and this preparation takes place in such a way that the last conclusion, the imparting of the mystery, does not pass from mouth to ear. At a definite point of time the pupil is so conditioned by preparation that the secret, the mystery, rises up before him. It does not need to be pronounced by a mouth, nor does it need to be heard by an ear; it must be born in the soul through what has passed between teacher and pupil.

There are no means of wringing from an Initiate the last things of the Mysteries, for no one can be compelled—by any means available on the physical plane—to betray with his mouth anything of the higher Mysteries. So it is with the higher Mysteries. And if that which should be born from the soul, as the higher Mysteries must be, were to be communicated to an unripe person through the mouth of another, it would be full of danger for this other person also. For he who had imparted the knowledge would be given completely into the power of his hearer for the rest of his incarnation. This, however, can never happen if the teacher simply prepares the pupil, and the pupil allows the truths to be born from out of his own soul.

When we know this, we understand that the original Gospel of Matthew could not be imparted without further preparation because men were not ripe to receive what was in it. For if Jerome, a Father of the Church, was himself not ripe for what it contained, then certainly other men were not. Those who were originally in possession of these communications, the Ebionites, did not impart them because, if received by unripe persons, they would have been so distorted that they must have led to what Jerome meant when he said that they would serve not for edification but for destruction. Now Jerome understood this; yet he allowed himself to impart in a certain way the Gospel of Matthew to the world. Hence we must realise that this Gospel has been imparted in a certain way and has had a corresponding effect upon the world. Now if we look round and see what influence it has had, then in the light of occult truths we shall find many things comprehensible. Who, standing on the ground of occultism, would care to say that all the persecutions and so on in the Christian world could be connected with the principles of Christ Jesus? Who, standing on the ground of occultism, would not say that into external evolution there must have flowed something not in accordance with Christian evolution? In short, a great misunderstanding must here exist.

We mentioned yesterday how on the ground of Christianity we should speak, for example, of Apollonius of Tyana; we set before us his greatness and significance and even called him an Adept. Yet when we go through early Christian literature we find everywhere accusations against Apollonius, as though everything he did, everything he accomplished, had been achieved only under the influence of the devil. There we have something that must be called misrepresentation, not only a misunderstanding of the personality and acts of Apollonius of Tyana. This is only one example among many. We understand it only when we see that the Gospels have been handed down in a way that must lead to misunderstandings, and that to-day, on the ground of occultism, our task is to go back to the true meaning of Christianity, concerning which the first teachers made many mistakes. It will then appear understandable that the next epoch of Christianity will be experienced differently from the earlier epochs. On the other hand, as already indicated, many things are stated here which can be said only because the listeners have taken part in the development of our Spiritual Science during the last few years, or are rightly disposed to enter into it: persons in whose souls there is a corresponding feeling and mood which will allow what is imparted to work upon them. Because souls have gone through at least one period of teaching, one incarnation, between the Mystery of Golgotha and the present time, the

Gospels can be spoken of to-day without fear that harm may result.

Thus we have before us the singular fact that the Gospels had to be communicated, but that Christianity could be understood only in its most imperfect form. Hence the Gospels have been subject to a method of research which can no longer determine what is historical and what is not, so that finally everything is denied. In their original form they must enter our hearts and souls, and this must give rise to a new power whereby the findings that will now be presented to men can be accepted by those who have been able worthily to feel the events from the Baptism of John to the Event of Golgotha.

An interpretation of the Christ-Event from the occult standpoint is thus a necessary preparation for the souls that in the near future are to experience something new, souls that are to look out on the world with new faculties. The old form of the Gospels will first receive its true value through our learning to read the Gospels with the aid of the Akashic record; through this alone will their full value be restored. In particular, the true significance of the Event of Golgotha can be fully demonstrated only by occult research. Only when the original significance of this Event is understood through occult research will the results it can have for human souls be recognised. Our task in the next few days will be to throw light, as far as is possible in one short lecture-cycle, on everything the human soul can experience under the influence of the Christ-Impulse, so that we may come to a deeper knowledge than was previously possible of all that took place in Palestine and on Golgotha.

LECTURE V

If you recall that in the course of our lectures we have come to look upon the Christ-Impulse as the most profound event in human evolution, you will doubtless agree that some exertion of our powers of mind and spirit is needed to understand its full meaning and range of influence. Certainly in the widest circles we find the bad habit of saying that the highest things in the world must be comprehensible in the simplest terms. If what someone is constrained to say about the sources of existence appears complicated, people turn away from it because 'the truth must be simple'. In the last resort it certainly is simple. But if at a certain stage we wish to learn to know the highest things, it is not hard to see that we must first clear the way to understanding them. And in order to enter into the full greatness, the full significance, of the Christ-Impulse, from a particular point of view, we must bring together many different matters.

We need only turn to the Pauline Epistles and we shall soon see that Paul, who sought especially to bring within range of human minds the supersensible nature of the Christ-Being, has drawn into the concept, the idea, of the Christ, the whole of human evolution, so to speak. If we let the Pauline Epistles work upon us, we have finally something which, through its extraordinary simplicity and through the deeply penetrating quality of the words and sentences, makes a most significant impression. But this is so only because Paul, through his own initiation, had worked his way up to that simplicity which is not the starting-point of what is true, but the consequence, the goal. If we wish to penetrate into what Paul was able finally to express in wonderful, monumental, simple words concerning the Christ-Being, we must come nearer to an understanding of human nature, for whose further development on Earth the Christ-Impulse came. Let us therefore consider what we already know concerning human nature, as shown through occult sight.

We divide the life of Man into two parts: the period between birth and death, and the period which runs its course between death and a new birth. Let us first of all look at man in his physical body. We know that occult sight sees him as a four-fold being, but as a four-fold being in process of development. Occult sight sees the physical body, etheric body, astral body and the Ego. We know that in order to understand human evolution we must learn the occult truth that this Ego, of which we become aware in our feelings and perceptions when we simply look away from the external world and try to live within ourselves, goes on from incarnation to incarnation. But we also know that this Ego is, as it were, ensheathed—although 'ensheathed' is not a good expression, we can use it for the present—by three other members of human nature, the astral body, the etheric body and the physical body. Of the astral body we know that in a certain respect it is the companion of the Ego through the various incarnations. For though during the Kamaloka time much of the astral body must be shed, it remains as a kind of force-body, which holds together the moral, intellectual and aesthetic progress we have stored up during an incarnation. Whatever constitutes true progress is held together by the power of the astral body, is carried from one incarnation to another, and is linked, as it were, with the Ego, which passes as the fundamentally eternal in us from incarnation to incarnation. Further, we know that from the etheric body, too, very much is cast off immediately after death, but an extract of this etheric body remains with us, an extract we take with us from one incarnation to another. In the first days directly after death we have before us a kind of backward review, like a great tableau, of our life up to that time, and we take with us a concentrated etheric extract. The rest of the etheric body is given over into the general etheric world in one form or another, according to the development of the person concerned.

When, however, we look at the fourth member of the human being, the physical body, it seems at first as if the physical body simply disappears into the physical world. One might say that this can be externally demonstrated, for to external sight the physical body is brought in one way or another to dissolution. The question, however, which everyone who occupies himself with Spiritual Science must put to himself is the following. Is not all that external physical cognition can tell us about the fate of our physical body perhaps only Maya? The answer does not lie very far away for anyone who has begun to understand Spiritual Science. When a man can say to himself, 'All that is offered by sense-appearance is Maya, external illusion', how can he think it really true that the physical body, delivered over to the grave or to the fire, disappears without trace, however crudely the appearance may obtrude on his senses? Perhaps, behind the external Maya, there lies something much deeper. Let us go further into this.

You will realise that in order to understand the evolution of the Earth, we must know the earlier embodiments of our planet; we must study the Saturn, Sun and Moon embodiments of the Earth. We know that the Earth has gone through its 'incarnations' just as every human being has done. Our physical body was prepared in the course of human evolution from the Saturn period of the Earth. With regard to the ancient Saturn time we cannot speak at all of etheric body, astral body and Ego in the sense of the present day. But the germ for the physical body was already sown, was embodied, during the Saturn evolution. During the Sun period of the Earth this germ was transformed, and then in this germ, in its altered form, the etheric was embodied. During the Moon period of the Earth the physical body was again transformed, and in it, and at the same time in the etheric body, which also came forth in an altered form, the astral body was incorporated. During the Earth period the Ego was incorporated. And is it conceivable that the part of us which was embodied during the Saturn period, our physical body, simply decomposes or is burned up and disappears into the elements, after the most significant endeavours had been made by divine-spiritual Beings through millions and millions of years, during the Saturn, Sun and Moon periods, in order to produce this physical body? If this were true, we should have before us the very remarkable fact that through three planetary stages, Saturn, Sun, Moon, a whole host of divine Beings worked to produce a cosmic element, such as our physical body is, and that during the Earth period this cosmic element is destined to vanish every time a person dies. It would be a remarkable drama if Maya —and external observation knows nothing else—were right. So now we ask: Can Maya be right?

At first it certainly seems as though occult knowledge declares Maya to be correct, for, strangely enough, occult knowledge seems in this case to harmonise with Maya. When we study the description given by spiritual knowledge of the development of man after death, we find that scarcely any notice is taken of the physical body. We are told that the physical body is thrown off, is given over to the elements of the Earth. We are told about the etheric body, the astral body, the Ego. The physical body is not further touched upon, and it seems as though the silence of spiritual knowledge were giving tacit assent to Maya-knowledge. So it seems, and in a certain way we are justified by Spiritual Science in speaking thus, for everything further must be left to a deeper grounding in Christology. For concerning what goes beyond Maya with regard to the physical body we cannot speak at all correctly unless the Christ-Impulse and everything connected with it has first been sufficiently explained.

If we observe how this physical body was experienced at

some definite moment in the past, we shall reach a quite remarkable result. Let us enquire into three kinds of folk-consciousness, three different forms of human consciousness concerning all that is connected with our physical body, during decisive periods in human evolution. We will enquire first of all among the Greeks.

We know that the Greeks were that remarkable people who rose to their highest development in the fourth post-Atlantean epoch of civilisation. We know that this epoch began about the eighth century before our era, and ended in the thirteenth, fourteenth and fifteenth centuries after the Event of Palestine. We can easily confirm what is said about this period from external information, traditions and documents. The first dimly clear accounts concerning Greece hardly go back farther than the sixth or seventh century before our era, though legendary accounts come down from still earlier times. We know that the greatness of the historical period of Greece has its source in the preceding period, the third post-Atlantean epoch. The inspired utterances of Homer reach back into the period preceding the fourth post-Atlantean epoch; and Aeschylus, who lived so early that a number of his works have been lost, points back to the drama of the Mysteries, of which he offers us but an echo. The third post-Atlantean epoch extends into the Greek age, but in that age the fourth epoch comes to full expression. The wonderful Greek culture is the purest expression of the fourth post-Atlantean epoch.

Now there falls upon our ear a remarkable saying from this land of Greece, a saying which permits us to see deeply into the soul of the man who felt himself truly a Greek, the saying of the hero*: 'Better a beggar in the upper world, than a king in the land of shades.' Here is a saying which betrays the deep susceptibility of the Greek soul. One might say that everything preserved to us of Greek classical beauty and classical greatness, of the gradual formation of the human

* Achilles, in the Odyssey.

ideal in the external world—all this resounds to us from that saying.

Let us recall the wonderful training of the human body in Greek gymnastics and in the great Games, which are only caricatured in these days by persons who understand nothing of what Greece really was. Every period has its own ideal, and we must keep this in mind if we want to understand how this development of the external physical body, as it stands there in its own form on the physical plane, was a peculiar privilege of the Greek spirit. So, too, was the creation of human ideals in plastic art, the enhancement of the human form in sculpture. And if we then look at the character of the Greek consciousness, as it held sway in a Pericles, for example, when a man had a feeling for the universally human and yet could stand firmly on his own feet and feel like a lord and king in the domain of his city—when we let all this work upon us, then we must say that the real love of the Greek was for the human form as it stood there before him on the physical plane, and that aesthetics, too, were turned to account in the development of this form. Where this human form was so well loved and understood, one could give oneself up to the thought: 'When that which gives to man this beautiful form on the physical plane is taken away from human nature, one cannot value the remainder as highly as the part destroyed by death.' This supreme love for the external form led unavoidably to a pessimistic view of what remains of man when he has passed through the gate of death. And we can fully understand that the Greek soul, having looked with so great a love upon the outer form, felt sad when compelled to think: 'This form is taken away from the human individuality. The human individuality lives on without this form!' If for the moment one looks at it solely from the point of view of feeling, then we must say: We have in Greece that branch of the human race which most loved and valued the human body, and underwent the deepest sorrow when the body perished in death.

Now let us consider another consciousness which developed about the same time, the Buddha consciousness, which had passed over from Buddha to his followers. There we have almost the opposite of the Greek attitude. We need only remember one thing: the kernel of the four great truths of Buddha is that human individuality is drawn by longing, by desire, into the existence where it is enshrouded by an external form. Into what kind of existence? Into an existence described in the Buddha-teaching as 'Birth is sorrow, sickness is sorrow, old age is sorrow, death is sorrow!' The underlying thought in this kernel of Buddhism is that by being enshrouded in an external bodily sheath, our individuality, which at birth comes down from divine-spiritual heights and returns to divine-spiritual heights at death, is exposed to the pain of existence, to the sorrow of existence. Only one way of salvation for men is expressed in the four great holy truths of Buddha: to become free from external existence, to throw off the external sheath. This means transforming the individuality so that it comes as soon as possible into a condition which will permit this throwing off. We note that the active feeling here is the reverse of the feeling dominant among the Greeks. Just as strongly as the Greek loved and valued the external bodily sheath, and felt the sadness of casting it aside, just as little did the adherent of Buddhism value it, regarding it as something to be cast aside as quickly as possible. And linked with this attitude was the struggle to overcome the craving for existence, an existence enshrouded by a bodily sheath.

Let us go a little more deeply into these Buddhist thoughts. A kind of theoretical view meets us in Buddhism concerning the succesive incarnations of man. It is not so much a question of what the individual thinks about the theory, as of what has penetrated into the consciousness of the adherents of Buddhism. I have often described this. I have said that we have perhaps no better opportunity of feeling what an adherent of Buddhism must have felt in regard to the continual incarnations of man, than by immersing ourselves in the traditional conversation between King Milinda and a Buddhist sage. 'Thou hast come in thy carriage: then reflect, O great King,' said the sage Nagasena, 'that all thou hast in the carriage is nothing but the wheels, the shaft, the body of the carriage and the seat, and beyond these nothing else exists except a word which covers wheels, shaft, body of carriage, seat, and so on. Thus thou canst not speak of a special individuality of the carriage, but thou must clearly understand that "carriage" is an empty word if thou thinkest of anything else than its parts, its members.' And another simile was chosen by Nagasena for King Milinda. 'Consider the almond-fruit which grows on the tree, and reflect that out of another fruit a seed was taken and laid in the earth and has decayed; out of that seed the tree has grown, and the almond-fruit upon it. Canst thou say that the fruit on the tree has anything else in common other than name and external form with the fruit from which the seed was taken and laid in the earth, where it decayed?' A man, Nagasena meant to say, has just as much in common with the man of his preceding incarnation as the almond-fruit on the tree has with the almond-fruit which, as seed, was laid in the earth. Anyone who believes that the form which stands before us as man, and is wafted away by death, is anything else than name and form, believes something as false as he who thinks that in the carriage—in the name 'carriage'—something else is contained than the parts of the carriage—the wheels, shaft, and so on. From the preceding incarnation nothing of what man calls his Ego passes over into the new incarnation.

That is important! And we must repeatedly emphasise that it is not to the point how this or that person chooses to interpret this or that saying of the Buddha, but how Buddhism worked in the consciousness of the people, what it gave to their souls. And what it gave to their souls is indeed expressed with intense clearness and significance in this parable of

King Milinda and the Buddhist sage. Of what we call the
'Ego', and of which we say that it is first felt and perceived by
man when he reflects upon his inner being, the Buddhist
says that fundamentally it is something that flows into him,
and belongs to Maya as much as everything else that does
not go from incarnation to incarnation.

I have elsewhere mentioned that if a Christian sage were
to be compared with the Buddhist one, he would have spoken
differently to King Milinda. The Buddhist said to the King:
'Consider the carriage, wheels, shaft, and so on; they are
parts of the carriage, and beyond these parts *carriage* is only
a name and form. With the word *carriage* thou hast named
nothing real in the carriage. If thou wilt speak of what is
real, thou must name the parts.' In the same case the Christian sage would have said: 'O wise King Milinda, thou hast
come in thy carriage; look at it! In it thou canst see only the
wheels, the shaft, the body of the carriage and so on, but I
ask thee now: Canst thou travel hither with the wheels only?
Or with the shaft only, or with the seat only? Thou canst not
travel hither on any of the separate *parts*. So far as they are
parts they make the carriage, but on the parts thou canst not
come hither. In order that the assembled parts can make the
carriage, something else is necessary than their being merely
parts. There must first be the quite definite thought of the
carriage, for it is this that brings together wheels, shaft, and
so on. And the thought of the carriage is something very
necessary: thou canst indeed not see the thought, but thou
must recognise it!'

The Christian sage would then turn to man and say:
'Of the individual person thou canst see only the external
body, the external acts and the external soul-experiences;
thou seest in man just as little of his Ego as in the name
carriage thou seest its separate parts. Something quite different is established within the parts, namely that which enables
thee to travel hither. So also in man: within all his parts
something quite different is established, namely that which

constitutes the Ego. The Ego is something real which as a
supersensible entity goes from one incarnation to another.'

How can we make a diagram of the Buddhist teaching of
reincarnation, so that it will represent the corresponding
Buddhist theory? With the circle we indicate a man between
birth and death. The man dies. The time when he dies is
marked by the point where the circle touches the line A–B.
Now what remains of all that has been spellbound within his
existence between birth and death? A summation of causes:

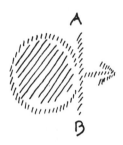

the results of acts, of everything a man has done, good or
bad, beautiful or ugly, clever or stupid. All that remains
over in this way works on as a set of causes, and so forms the

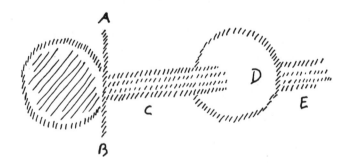

causal nucleus (C) for the next incarnation. Round this
causal nucleus new body-sheaths (D) are woven for the next
incarnation. These body-sheaths go through new experiences,
as did the body-sheaths around the earlier causal nucleus.

From these experiences there remains again a causal nucleus
(E). It includes experiences that have come into it from
earlier incarnations, together with experiences from its last
life. Hence it serves as the causal nucleus for the next incarnation, and so on. This means that what goes through the
incarnations consists of nothing but causes and effects.
There is no continuing Ego to connect the incarnations;
nothing but causes and effects working over from one
incarnation into the next. So when in this incarnation I call
myself an 'Ego', this is not because the same Ego was there
in the preceding incarnation. What I call my Ego is only a
Maya of the present incarnation.

Anyone who really knows Buddhism must picture it in this
way, and he must clearly understand that what we call the
Ego has no place in Buddhism. Now let us go on to what we
know through anthroposophical cognition.

How has man ever been able to develop his Ego? Through
the Earth-evolution. Only in the course of the Earth-evolution has he reached the stage of developing his Ego. It was
added to his physical body, etheric body and astral body on
the Earth. Now, if we remember all we had to say concerning
the evolutionary phases of man during the Saturn, Sun and
Moon periods, we know that during the Moon period the
human physical body had not yet acquired a quite definite
form; it received this first on Earth. Hence we speak of the
Earth-existence as the epoch in which the Spirits of Form
first took part, and metamorphosed the physical body of
man so that it has its present form. This forming of the
human physical body was necessary if the Ego were to find
a place in man. The physical Earth-body, set down on the
physical Earth, provided the foundation for the dawn of the
Ego as we know it. If we keep this in mind, what follows will
no longer seem incomprehensible.

With regard to the valuation of the Ego among the
Greeks, we saw that for them it was expressed externally in
the human form. Let us now recall that Buddhism, according

to its knowledge, sets out to overcome and cast off as quickly as possible the external form of the human physical body. Can we then wonder that in Buddhism we find no value attached to anything connected with this bodily form? It is the essence of Buddhism to value the external form of the physical body as little as it values the external form which the Ego needs in order to come into being: indeed, all this is completely set aside. Buddhism lost the form of the Ego through the way in which it undervalued the physical body.

Thus we see how these two spiritual currents are polarically opposed: the Greek current, which set the highest value on the external form of the physical body as the external form of the Ego, and Buddhism, which requires that the external form of the physical body, with all craving after existence, shall be overcome as soon as possible, so that in its theory it has completely lost the Ego.

Between these two opposite world-philosophies stands ancient Hebraism. Ancient Hebraism is far from thinking so poorly of the Ego as Buddhism does. In Buddhism, it is heresy to recognise a continuous Ego, going on from one incarnation to the next. But ancient Hebraism held very strongly to this so-called heresy, and it would never have entered the mind of an adherent of that religion to suppose that his personal divine spark, with which he connected his concept of the Ego, is lost when he goes through the gate of death. If we want to make clear how the ancient Hebrew regarded the matter, we must say that he felt himself connected in his inner being with the Godhead, intimately connected; he knew that through the finest threads of his soul-life, as it were, he was dependent on the being of this Godhead.

With regard to the concept of the Ego, the ancient Hebrew was quite different from the Buddhist, but in another respect he was also very different from the Greek. When we survey those ancient times as a whole, we find that the estimation of human personality, and hence that valuation of the external human form which was peculiar to the Greek, is not present in ancient Hebraism. For the Greek it would have been absolute nonsense to say: 'Thou shalt not make to thyself any image of thy God.' He would not have understood if someone had said to him: 'Thou shalt not make to thyself any image of thy Zeus, or thy Apollo.' For he felt that the highest thing was the external form, and that the highest tribute a man could offer to the Gods was to clothe them with this human form which he himself valued so much. Nothing would have seemed more absurd to him than the commandment: 'Thou shalt make to thyself no image of God.' As artist, the Greek gave his human form to his gods. He thought of himself as made in the likeness of the Divine, and he carried out his contests, his wrestling, his gymnastics and so on, in order to become a real copy of the God.

But the ancient Hebrew had the commandment, 'Thou shalt make to thyself no image of God!' This was because he did not value the external form as the Greeks had done; he regarded it as unworthy in relation to the Divine. The ancient Hebrew was as far removed on the one side from the disciple of Buddhism, who would have much preferred to cast off the human form entirely on passing through death, as he was on the other side from the Greek. He was mindful of the fact that it was this form that gave expression to the commands, the laws, of the Divine Being, and he clearly understood that a 'righteous man' handed down through the following generations what he, as a righteous man, had gathered together. Not the extinguishing of the form, but the handing on of the form through the generations was what concerned the ancient Hebrew. His point of view stood midway between that of the Buddhist, who had lost the value of the Ego, and that of the Greek, who saw in the form of the body the very highest, and felt it as sorrowful when the bodily form had to disappear with death.

So these three views stand over against one another. And

for a closer understanding of ancient Hebraism we must
make it clear that what the Hebrew valued as his Ego was in
a certain sense also the Divine Ego. The God lived on in
humanity, lived within man. In his union with the God, the
Hebrew felt at the same time his own Ego, and felt it to be
coincident with the Divine Ego. The Divine Ego sustained
him; the Divine Ego was active within him. The Greek said:
'I value my Ego so greatly that I look with horror on what will
happen to it after death.' The Buddhist said: 'That which is
the cause of the external form of man must fall away from
man as soon as possible.' The Hebrew said: 'I am united
with God; that is my fate, and as long as I am united with
Him I bear my fate. I know nothing else than the identifica-
tion of my Ego with the Divine Ego.'

This old Judaic mode of thought, standing midway between Greek thought and Buddhism, does not involve, as
Greek thought does from the outset, a predisposition to
tragedy in face of the phenomenon of death, but tragic feeling is indirectly present in it. It is truly Greek for the hero to
say: 'Better a beggar in the upper world'—i.e. with the
human bodily form—'than a king in the realm of shades',
but a Hebrew could not have said it without something
more. For the Hebrew knows that when in death his bodily
form falls away, he remains united with God. He cannot
fall into a tragic mood simply through the fact of death.
Still, the predisposition to tragedy is present indirectly in
ancient Hebraism, and is expressed in the most wonderfully
dramatic story ever written in ancient times, the story of Job.

We see there how the Ego of Job feels bound up with his
God, how it comes into conflict with his God, but differently
from the way in which the Greek Ego comes into conflict.
We are shown how misfortune after misfortune falls upon
Job, although he is conscious that he is a righteous man and
has done all he can to maintain the connection of his Ego
with the Divine Ego. And while it seems that his existence is
blessed and ought to be blessed, a tragic fate breaks over him.

Job is not aware of any sin; he is conscious that he has acted as a righteous man must act towards his God. Word is brought to him that all his possessions have been destroyed. all his family slain. Then his external body, this divine form, is stricken with grievous disease. There he stands, the man who can consciously say to himself: "Through the inward connection I feel with my God, I have striven to be righteous before my God. My fate, decreed to me by this God, has placed me in the world. It is the acts of this God which have fallen so heavily upon me." And his wife stands there beside him, and calls upon him in strange words to deny his God. These words are handed down correctly. They are one of the sayings which correspond exactly with the Akashic record: 'Renounce thy God, since thou hast to suffer so much, since He has brought these sufferings upon thee, and die!' What endless depth lies in these words: Lose the consciousness of the connection with thy God; then thou wilt fall out of the Divine connection, like a leaf from the tree, and thy God can no longer punish thee! But loss of the connection with God is at the same time death! For as long as the Ego feels itself connected with God, death cannot touch it. The Ego must first tear itself away from connection with God; then only can death touch it.

According to outward appearance everything is against righteous Job; his wife sees his suffering and advises him to renounce God and die; his friends come and say: 'You must have done this or that, for God never punishes a righteous man.' But he is aware, as far as his personal consciousness is concerned, that he has done nothing unrighteous. Through the events he encounters in the external world he stands before an immense tragedy: the tragedy of not being able to understand human existence, of feeling himself bound up with God and not understanding how what he is experiencing can have its source in God.

Let us think of all this lying with its full weight upon a human soul. Let us think of this soul breaking forth into the

words which have come down to us from the traditional
story of Job: 'I know that my Redeemer liveth! I know that
one day I shall again be clothed with my bones, with my
skin, and that I shall look upon God with whom I am
united.' This consciousness of the indestructibility of the
human individuality breaks forth from the soul of Job in
spite of all the pain and suffering. So powerful is the consciousness of the Ego as the inner content of the ancient
Hebrew belief! But here we meet with something in the
highest degree remarkable. 'I know that my Redeemer
liveth,' says Job, 'I know that one day I shall again be
covered with my skin, and that with mine eyes I shall behold
the glory of my God.' Job brings into connection with the
Redeemer-thought the external body, skin and bones, eyes
which see physically. Strange! Suddenly, in this consciousness that stands midway between Greek thought and
Buddhism—this ancient Hebrew consciousness—we meet a
consciousness of the significance of the physical bodily form
in connection with the Redeemer-thought, which then
becomes the foundation, the basis, for the Christ-thought.
And when we take the answer of Job's wife, still more light
falls on everything Job says. 'Renounce thy God and die.'
This signifies that he who does not renounce his God does not
die. That is implied in these words. But then, what does
'die' mean? To die means to throw off the physical body.
External Maya seems to say that the physical body passes
over into the elements of the earth, and, so to speak, disappears. Thus in the answer of Job's wife there lies the following: 'Do what is necessary that thy physical body may
disappear!' It could not mean anything else, or the words of
Job that follow would have no sense. For man can understand anything only if he can understand the means whereby
God has placed us in the world; if, that is, he can understand
the significance of the physical body. And Job himself says,
for this too lies in his words: 'O, I know full well that I need
not do anything that would bring about the complete

disappearance of my physical body, for that would be only an external appearance. There is a possibility that my body may be saved, because my Redeemer liveth. This I cannot express otherwise than in the words: My skin, my bones, will one day be re-created. With my eyes I shall behold the Glory of my God. I can lawfully keep my physical body, but for this I must have the consciousness that my Redeemer liveth.'

So in this story of Job there comes before us for the first time a connection between the Form of the physical body, which the Buddhist would strip off, which sadly the Greek sees pass away, and the Ego-consciousness. We meet for the first time with something like a prospect of deliverance for that which the host of Gods from ancient Saturn, Sun and Moon, down to the Earth itself, have brought forth as the Form of the physical body. And if the Form is to be preserved, if we are to say of it that what has been given us of bones, skin and sense-organs is to have an outcome, then we must add: 'I know that my Redeemer liveth.'

This is strange, someone might now say. Does it really follow from the story of Job that Christ awakens the dead and rescues the bodily Form which the Greeks believed would disappear? And is there perhaps anything in the story to indicate that for the general evolution of humanity it is not right, in the full sense of the word, that the external bodily Form should disappear completely? May it not be interwoven with the whole human evolutionary process? Has this connection a part to play in the future? Does it depend upon the Christ-Being?

These questions are set before us. And they mean that we shall have to widen in a certain connection what we have so far learnt from Spiritual Science. We know that when we pass through the gate of death we retain at least the etheric body, but we strip off the physical body entirely; we see it delivered up to the elements. But its Form, which has been worked upon through millions and millions of years—is that lost in nothingness, or is it in some way retained?

We will consider this question in the light of the explanations you have heard to-day, and to-morrow we will approach it by asking: How is the impulse given to human evolution by the Christ related to the significance of the external physical body—that body which throughout Earth evolution is consigned to the grave, the fire or the air, although the preservation of its Form is necessary for the future of mankind?

LECTURE VI

By taking our start from what was said yesterday, we shall be able to come nearer to the fundamental questions of Christianity and to penetrate into its essential nature. We shall see that only by this means can we see into the heart of what the Christ-Impulse has become for the evolution of humanity and what it will become in the future.

People are always insisting that the answers to the highest questions must not be complicated; the truth must be brought directly to each person in the simplest way. In support of this they argue, for example, that the Apostle John in his last years expressed the quintessence of Christianity in words of truth: 'Children, love one another.' No one, however, should conclude that a person who simply pronounces the words, 'Children, love one another', knows the essence of Christianity and of all truth for men. Before the Apostle John was entitled to pronounce these words, he had fulfilled various preconditions. We know it was at the end of a long life, in his ninety-fifth year, that he came to this utterance; only by then, in that particular incarnation, had he earned the right to use such words. Indeed, he stands there as a witness that this saying, if it came from any chance individual, would not have the power it had from him. For he had achieved something else also. Although the critics dispute it, he was the author of the John Gospel, the Apocalypse and the Epistles of John. Throughout his life he had not always said, 'Children, love one another!' He had written a work which belongs to the most difficult productions of man, the Apocalypse, and the John Gospel, which penetrates most intimately and deeply into the human soul. He had gained the right to pronounce such a saying only through a long

life and through what he had accomplished. If anyone lives
a life such as his, and does what he did, and then says, as he
did, 'Children, love one another!' there are no grounds for
objecting to it. We must, however, be quite clear that although some things can be compressed into a few words, so
that these few words signify very much, the same few words
may also say nothing. Many a person who pronounces a
word of wisdom, which in its proper setting would perhaps
signify something very deep, believes that by merely uttering
it he has said a very great deal.

The writer of the Apocalypse and of the John Gospel, in
his greatest age, could speak the words 'Children, love one
another!' out of the essence of Christianity, but the same
words from the mouth of another person may be a mere
phrase. We must gather matters for the understanding of
Christianity from far afield, so that we may apply them to
the simplest truths of daily life.

Yesterday we had to approach the question, so fateful for
modern thought: What are we to make of the physical body
in relation to the four-fold being of man?

We shall see how the points brought out yesterday in
looking at the differing views of the Greeks, the ancient
Hebrews and the Buddhists will lead us further towards understanding the nature of Christianity. But if we are to learn
more concerning the fate of the physical body, we must first
take up a question which is central to the whole Christian
cosmic conception; a question which lies at the very core of
Christianity: How it is with the Resurrection of Christ? Must
we not assume that for the understanding of Christianity it
is essential to reach an understanding of the Resurrection?

To see how important this is, we need only recall a
passage in the first Epistle of Paul to the Corinthians, (I
Corinthians XV: 14–20):

If Christ has not been raised, then our preaching is in vain,
and your faith is in vain. We are even found to be mis-

representing God, because we testified of God that he raised Christ, whom he did not raise if it is true that the dead are not raised. For if the dead are not raised, then Christ has not been raised. If Christ has not been raised, your faith is futile and you are still in your sins. Then those also who have fallen asleep in Christ have perished. If in this life we who are in Christ have only hope, we are of all men most to be pitied. But in fact Christ has been raised from the dead, the first fruits of those who have fallen asleep.*

We must remember that Christianity, in so far as it has extended over the world, began with Paul. And if we are disposed to take these important words seriously, we cannot simply pass them over by saying that we must leave the question of the Resurrection unexplained. For what is it that Paul says? That the whole of Christianity has no justification, and the whole Christian Faith no meaning, if the Resurrection is not true! That is what is said by Paul, with whom Christianity as a fact of history had its starting-point. And it means that anyone who is willing to give up the Resurrection must give up Christianity as Paul understood it.

And now let us pass over almost two thousand years and ask people of the present day how, according to the requirements of modern culture, they stand with regard to the question of the Resurrection. I shall not now take note of those who simply deny Jesus entirely; it is naturally quite easy for them to be clear regarding the question of the Resurrection. If Jesus never lived, one need not trouble about the Resurrection. Leaving such persons aside, we will turn to those who about the middle or in the last third of the nineteenth century had accepted the current ideas of our time—the time in which we are still living. We will ask them what they think, in comformity with the whole culture of our day, concerning the question of the Resurrection.

* Quotations from the New Testament are in the Revised Standard Version, 1946.

We will take a man who has gained great influence over the way of thinking of those who consider themselves best informed—David Friedrich Strauss. In his work on Reimarus, a thinker of the eighteenth century, we read: 'The Resurrection of Jesus is really a shibboleth, concerning which not only the various conceptions of Christianity, but the various world-philosophies and stages of spiritual evolution, are at variance.' And in a Swiss journal almost of the same date we read: 'As soon as I can convince myself of the reality of the Resurrection of Christ, this absolute miracle, I tear down the modern conception of the world. This breach in what I believe to be the inviolable order of Nature would make an irreparable rent in my system, in my whole thought-world.'

Let us ask how many persons of our present time who, according to the modern standpoint, must and do subscribe to these words, would say, 'If I were obliged to recognise the Resurrection as historical fact, I would tear down my whole system of thought, philosophical or otherwise.' Let us ask how should the Resurrection, as historical fact, fit in with a modern man's outlook on the world.

Let us recall something indicated in my first public lecture on this subject, that the Gospels are to be taken first and foremost as Initiation writings. The leading events depicted in the Gospels are fundamentally Initiation events—events which had formerly taken place within the secret places of the temples of the Mysteries, when this or that person, who had been deemed worthy, was initiated by the hierophants. Such a person, after he had been prepared for a long time, went through a kind of death and a kind of resurrection. He had also to go through certain situations in life which reappear for us in the Gospels—in the story of the Temptation, the story set on the Mount of Olives, and other similar ones. That is why the accounts of ancient Initiates, which do not aim to be biographies in the usual sense, show such resemblance to the Gospel stories of Christ Jesus. And when we read the history of the greatest initiates, of Apollonius of Tyana, or indeed even of Buddha or Zarathustra, or the life of Osiris or of Orpheus, it often seems that important characteristics of their lives are the same as those narrated of Christ Jesus in the Gospels. But although we must grant that we have to seek in the Initiation ceremonies of the old Mysteries for the prototypes of important events narrated in the Gospels, on the other hand we see quite clearly that the great teachings of the life of Christ Jesus are saturated throughout with individual details which are not intended as a mere repetition of Initiation ceremonies, but make it very plain that what is described is actual fact. Must we not say that we receive a remarkably factual impression when the following is pictured for us in the Gospel of John XX: 1–10:

Now on the first day of the week Mary Magdalene came to the tomb early, while it was still dark, and saw that the stone had been taken away from the tomb. So she ran, and went to Simon Peter and the other disciple, the one whom Jesus loved, and said to them, 'They have taken the Lord out of the tomb, and we do not know where they have laid him.' Peter then came out with the other disciple, and they went towards the tomb. They both ran, but the other disciple outran Peter and reached the tomb first; and stooping to look in, he saw the linen cloths lying there, but he did not go in. Then Simon Peter came, following him, and he went into the tomb; he saw the linen cloths lying, and the napkins, which had been on his head, not lying with the linen cloths but rolled up in a place by itself. Then the other disciple, who reached the tomb first, also went in, and he saw and believed; for as yet they did not know the scripture, that he must rise from the dead. Then the disciples went back to their homes.

But Mary stood weeping outside the tomb, and as she wept she stooped to look into the tomb; and she saw two angels in white, sitting where the body of Jesus had lain, one at the head and one at the feet. They said to her, 'Woman, why are you weeping?' She said to them, 'Because they have taken away my Lord, and I do not know where they have laid him.' Saying this, she turned and saw Jesus standing, but she did not know that it was Jesus. Jesus said to her, 'Woman, why are you weeping? Whom do you seek?' Supposing him to be the gardener, she said to him, 'Sir, if you have carried him away, tell me where you have laid him and I will take him away.' Jesus said to her, 'Mary.' She turned and said to him in Hebrew, 'Rab-boni!' (which means Teacher). Jesus said to her, 'Do not hold me, for I have not yet ascended to the Father; but go to my brethren and say to them, I am ascending to my Father and your Father, to my God and your God.'

Here is a situation described in such detail that if we wish to picture it in imagination there is hardly anything lacking —when, for example, it is said that the one disciple runs faster than the other, or that the napkin which had covered the head was laid aside in another place, and so on. In every detail something is described which would have no meaning if it did not refer to a fact. Attention was drawn on a former occasion to one detail, that Mary did not recognise Christ Jesus, and we asked how was it possible that after three days anyone could fail to recognise in the same form a person previously known. Hence we had to note that Christ appeared to Mary in a changed form, or these words would have no meaning.

Here, therefore, a distinction must be kept in mind. First, we have to understand the Resurrection as a translation into historic fact of the awakening that took place in the holy Mysteries of all times, only with the difference that he who in the Mysteries raised up the individual pupil was the hierophant; while the Gospels indicate that He who raised up Christ is the Being whom we designate as the Father—

that the Father Himself raised up the Christ. Here we are shown that what had formerly been carried out on a small scale in the depths of the Mysteries was now and once for all enacted for humanity by Divine Spirits, and that the Being who is designated as the Father acted as hierophant in the raising to life of Christ Jesus. Thus we have here, enhanced to the highest degree, something which formerly had taken place on a small scale in the Mysteries.

That is the first point. The other is that, interwoven with matters which carry us back to the Mysteries, there are descriptions so detailed that even to-day we can reconstruct from the Gospels the situations even to their minute particulars, as we have just seen in the passage read to you. But this passage includes one detail that calls for particular attention. There must be a meaning in the words, 'For they did not as yet know the Scripture, that He must rise from the dead. Then the disciples went back to their homes.' Let us ask: Of what had the disciples been able so far to convince themselves? It is described as clearly as anything can be that the linen wrappings are there, but the body is not there, is no longer in the grave. The disciples had not been able to convince themselves of anything else, and they understood nothing else when they now went home. Otherwise the words have no meaning. The more deeply you enter into the text, the more you must say that the disciples who were standing by the grave were convinced that the linen wrappings were there, but that the body was no longer in the grave. They went home with the thought: 'Where has the body gone? Who has taken it out of the grave?'

And now, from the conviction that the body is not there, the Gospels lead us slowly to the events through which the disciples were finally convinced of the Resurrection. How were they convinced? Through the fact that, as the Gospels relate, Christ appeared to them by degrees, so that they could say, 'He is there!', and this went so far that Thomas, called the Doubter, could lay his finger in the prints of the wounds.

In short, we can see from the Gospels that the disciples became convinced of the Resurrection through Christ having
come to them after it as the Risen One. The proof for the
disciples was that He was there. And if these disciples, who
had gradually come to the conviction that Christ was alive,
although He had died, had been asked what they actually
believed, they would have said: 'We have proofs that Christ
lives.' But they certainly would not have spoken as Paul
spoke later, after he had gone through his experience on the
road to Damascus.

Anyone who allows the Gospels and the Pauline Epistles
to work upon him will notice the deep underlying difference
between the fundamental tone of the Gospels as regards the
understanding of the Resurrection, and the Pauline conception of it. Paul, indeed, draws a parallel between his conviction of the Resurrection and that of the Gospels, for in
saying 'Christ is risen', he indicates that Christ, after He had
been crucified, appeared as a living Being to Cephas, to the
Twelve, then to five hundred brethren at one time; and last
of all to himself, Paul, as to one born out of due time, Christ
had appeared from out of the fiery glory of the Spiritual.
Christ had appeared to the disciples also; Paul refers to that,
and the events lived through with the Risen One were the
same for Paul as they had been for the disciples. But what
Paul immediately joins to these, as the outcome for him of the
event of Damascus, is his wonderful and easily comprehensible theory of the Being of Christ.

What, from the event of Damascus onwards, was the
Being of Christ for Paul? The Being of Christ was for him the
'Second Adam'; and he immediately differentiates between
the first Adam and the second Adam, the Christ. He calls
the first Adam the progenitor of men on Earth because
he sees in him the first man, from whom all other men are
descended. For Paul, it is Adam who has bequeathed to
human beings the body which they carry about with them as
a physical body. All men have inherited their physical body

from Adam. This is the body which meets us in external Maya, and is mortal; it is the body inherited from Adam, the corruptible body, the physical body of man that decays in death. With this body men are 'clothed'. The second Adam, Christ, is regarded by Paul as possessing, in contrast to the first, the incorruptible, the immortal body. Paul then affirms that through Christian evolution men are gradually made ready to put on the second Adam in place of the first Adam; the incorruptible body of the second Adam, Christ, in place of the corruptible body of the first Adam. What Paul seems to require of all who call themselves true Christians is something that violates all the old conceptions of the world. As the first corruptible body is descended from Adam, so must the incorruptible body originate from the second Adam, from Christ. Every Christian could say: 'Because I am descended from Adam, I have a corruptible body as Adam had; but in that I set myself in the right relationship to Christ, I receive from Him, the second Adam, an incorruptible body.' For Paul, this view shines out directly from the experience of Damascus. We can perhaps express what Paul wishes to say by means of a simple diagram:

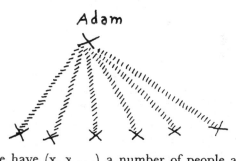

Here we have (x, x . . .) a number of people at a given time. Paul would trace them all back to the first Adam, from whom they are all descended and by whom they are given the corruptible body. According to Paul's conception, however, something else is possible. Just as human beings can say, 'We are related because we are all descended from the one progenitor, Adam,' so they can say, 'As without any action of ours, through the relationships of human generation lines can be traced back to Adam, so it is possible for us to cause something else to arise within us; something that could make us different beings. Just as the natural lines lead back to Adam, so it must be possible to represent lines which lead, not to the corruptible body of the fleshly Adam, but to the body that is incorruptible. Through our relationship to Christ, we can—according to the Pauline view—bear this incorruptible body within us, just as through Adam we bear the corruptible body.'

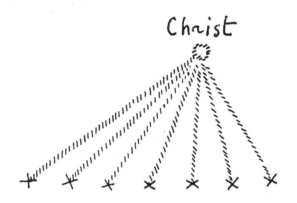

There is nothing more uncomfortable for the modern consciousness than this idea. For looking at the matter quite soberly, what does it demand from us? It demands something which, for modern thought, is really monstrous. Modern thought has long disputed whether all human beings are descended from one primeval human being, but it may be allowed that all are descended from a single human being who was the first on earth as regards physical consciousness. Paul, however, demands the following. He says: 'If you desire to be a Christian in the true sense, you must conceive that within you something can arise which can live in you, and from which you can draw spiritual lines to a second

Adam, to Christ, to that very Christ who on the third day
rose from the grave, just as all men can trace lines back to the
physical body of the first Adam.' So Paul demands that all
who call themselves Christians should cause something
within them to arise; something leading to that entity which
on the third day rose out of the grave in which the body of
Christ Jesus had been laid. Anyone who does not grant this
cannot come into any relationship with Paul; he cannot say
he understands Paul. If man, as regards his corruptible
body, is descended from the first Adam, then, by receiving
the Being of Christ into his own being, he has the possibility
of having a second ancestor. This ancestor, however, is He
who, on the third day after His body had been laid in the
earth, rose out of the grave.

Let us clearly understand that Paul makes this demand,
however displeasing it may be to modern thinkers. From this
Pauline statement we will indeed approach the modern
thinker; but one ought not to have any other opinion concerning that which meets us so clearly in the Pauline
writings; one ought not to twist the meaning of something so
clearly expressed by Paul. Certainly it is pleasant to interpret
something allegorically and to say it was meant in such and
such a way; but all these interpretations make no sense.
If we wish to connect a meaning with the Pauline statement
we are bound to say—even if modern consciousness regards
it as superstition—that, according to Paul, Christ rose from
the dead after three days.

Let us go further. An assertion such as this, made by Paul
after he had reached the summit of his initiation through the
event of Damascus—the assertion concerning the second
Adam and His rising from the grave—could be made only by
someone whose whole mode of thought and outlook had
been derived from Greek thought; by one whose roots were
in Greece, even if he were also a Hebrew; by one who in a
certain respect had brought all his Hebraism as an offering
to the Greek mind. For, if we come closer to all this, what is

it that Paul really declares? Looking with inner vision on
that which the Greeks loved and valued, the external form of
the human body, concerning which they had the tragic
feeling that it comes to an end when the individual passes
through the gate of death, Paul says: 'With the Resurrection
of Christ, the body has been raised in triumph from the
grave.' If we are to build a bridge between these two world-
outlooks, we can best do it in the following way.

The Greek hero said from his Greek feeling: 'Better a
beggar in the upper world than a king in the land of shades.'
He said this because he was convinced that the external form
of the physical body, so highly cherished by the Greeks, was
lost for ever in passing through the gate of death. On this
same soil, out of which this tragic mood of intoxication with
beauty had grown, Paul appeared, he who first proclaimed
the Gospel to the Greeks. We do not deviate from his words
if we translate them as follows: 'That which you value
above all, the human bodily form, will no longer be destroyed. Christ is risen as the first of those who are raised
from the dead! The Form of the physical body is not lost,
but is given back to humanity through the Resurrection of
Christ!' That which the Greeks valued most highly was given
back to them with the Resurrection by Paul the Jew, who
had been steeped in Greek culture. Only a Greek would so
think and speak, but only someone who had become a
Greek with all the preconceptions derived from his Jewish
ancestry. Only a Jew who had become a Greek could speak
in this way; no one else.

But how can we approach these things from the standpoint of Spiritual Science? For we have reached the point of
knowing that Paul demands something which thoroughly
upsets the calculations of the modern thinker. Let us endeavour from the standpoint of Spiritual Science to get
nearer to what Paul demands. Let us collect what we know
from Spiritual Science, so as to bring an idea to meet Paul's
statement.

When we review the very simplest spiritual-scientific truths, we know that man consists of physical body, etheric body, astral body and Ego. If now you ask someone who has studied Spiritual Science a little, but not very thoroughly, whether he knows the physical body of man, he will be sure to answer: 'I know it quite well, for I see it when a person stands before me. The other members are supersensible, invisible, and one cannot see them, but the physical human body I know very well.' Is it really the physical body of man that appears before our eyes when we meet a man with our ordinary vision? I ask you, who without clairvoyant vision has ever seen a physical human body? What is it that people have before them if they see only with physical eyes and physical understanding? A human body, but one consisting of physical body, etheric body, astral body and Ego. And when a man stands before us, it is as an organised assembly of physical body, etheric body, astral body and Ego. It would make as little sense to say that a physical body stood before us as it would if, when giving someone a glass of water, we were to say, 'There is hydrogen in that glass.' Water consists of hydrogen and oxygen, as man consists of physical, etheric and astral bodies, and Ego. Their assemblage is visible, just as water is, but the hydrogen and oxygen are not. Anyone who said he saw hydrogen in the water would be obviously mistaken. So is anyone who thinks he sees the physical body when he sees a man in the external world. What he normally sees is not a physical human body, but a four-membered being. He sees the physical body only in so far as it is permeated by the other members of the human being. And it is then changed in the same way that hydrogen is changed when it is permeated with oxygen in water. For hydrogen is a gas, and oxygen also; from the two gases united we get a liquid. Why should it be incomprehensible that the man who meets us in the physical world is quite unlike his single members, the physical, etheric and astral bodies and the Ego, just as water is quite unlike hydrogen? And so he is!

Hence we cannot rely upon the Maya which appears to us as the physical body. We must think of the physical body in a quite different way if we want to draw nearer to its nature.

The observation of the physical human body, in itself, belongs to the most difficult clairvoyant problems, the hardest of all! Suppose we allow the external world to perform on man the experiment which is similar to the disintegration of water into hydrogen and oxygen. In death this experiment is performed by the great world. We then see how man lays aside his physical body. But does he really lay aside his physical body? The question seems absurd, for what could be clearer than the apparent fact that at death man lays aside his physical body? But what is it that he lays aside? It is something no longer imbued with the physical body's most important possession during life: its Form. Directly after death the Form begins to withdraw from the dead body. We are left with decaying substances, no longer characterised by the Form. The body laid aside is composed of substances and elements which we can trace also in Nature; in the natural order of things they would not produce a human Form. Yet this Form belongs quite essentially to the physical human body. To ordinary clairvoyance it seems evident that at death a person simply discards these material substances, which are then handed over to decay or burning, and that nothing of the physical body is left. The clairvoyant then observes how after death the Ego, astral body and etheric body remain connected during the person's review of his past life. Then he sees how the etheric body separates itself, how an extract of it remains, while the main portion dissolves in one way or another into the general cosmic ether. It does indeed seem that the person has laid aside his physical body, with its substances and forces, and then, after a few days, the etheric body. When the clairvoyant follows the person further through the Kamaloka period, he sees how an extract of the astral body goes with him during the

life between death and a new birth, while the rest of the
astral body is given over to the cosmic astrality.

So we see that physical, etheric and astral bodies are laid
aside, and that the physical body seems to drain away completely into materials and forces which, through decay or
burning or some other form of dissolution, are returned to
the elements. But the more clairvoyance is developed in our
time, the clearer will it be that the physical forces and substances laid aside are not the whole physical body, for its
complete configuration could never derive from them alone.
To these substances and forces there belongs something else,
best called the 'Phantom' of the man. This Phantom is the
Form-shape which as a spiritual texture works up the
physical substances and forces so that they fill out the Form
which we encounter as the man on the physical plane. The
sculptor can bring no statue into existence if he merely takes
marble or something else, and strikes away wildly so that
single pieces spring off just as the substance permits. As the
sculptor must have the 'thought' which he impresses on the
substance, so is a 'thought' related to the human body: not in
the same way as the thought of the artist, for the material of
the human body is not marble or plaster, but as a real
thought, the Phantom, in the external world. Just as the
thought of the plastic artist is stamped upon his material, so
the Phantom of the physical body is stamped upon the
substances of the earth which we see given over after death
to the grave or the fire. The Phantom belongs to the physical
body as its enduring part, a more important part than the
external substances. The external substances are merely
loaded into the network of the human Form, as one might
load apples into a cart. You can see how important the
Phantom is. The substances which fall asunder after death
are essentially those we meet externally in nature. They are
merely caught up by the human Form.

If you think more deeply, can you believe that all the work
of the great Divine Spirits though the Saturn, Sun and

Moon periods has merely created something which is handed over at death to the elements of the Earth? No—that which was developed during the Saturn, Sun and Moon periods is not the physical body that is laid aside at death. It is the Phantom, the Form, of the physical body. We must be quite clear that to understand the physical body is not an easy thing. Above all, this understanding must not be sought for in the world of illusion, the world of Maya. We know that the foundation, the germ, of this Phantom of the physical body was laid down by the Thrones during the Saturn period; during the Sun period the Spirits of Wisdom worked further upon it, the Spirits of Movement during the Moon period, and the Spirits of Form during the Earth period. And it is only in this period that the physical body received the Phantom. We call these Spirits the Spirits of Form, because they really live in the Phantom of the physical body. So in order to understand the physical body, we must go back to the Phantom.

If we look back to the beginning of our Earth-existence, we can say that the hosts from the ranks of the higher Hierarchies who had prepared the physical human body in its own proper Form during the Saturn, Sun and Moon periods, up to the Earth period, had from the outset placed this Phantom within the Earth evolution. In fact the Phantom, which cannot be seen with the physical eye, was what was first there of the physical body of man. It is a transparent body of force. What the physical eye sees are the physical substances which a person eats and takes into himself, and they fill out the invisible Phantom. If the physical eye looks upon a physical body, what it sees is the mineral part that fills the physical body, not the physical body itself. But how has this mineral part found its way into the Phantom of man's physical body? To answer this question, let us picture once more the genesis, the first 'becoming', of man on Earth.

From Saturn, Sun and Moon there came over that network of forces which in its true form meets us as the invisible

Phantom of the physical body. For a higher clairvoyance it appears as Phantom only when we look away from all the external substance that fills it out. This is the Phantom which stands at the starting-point of man's Earth existence, when he was invisible as a physical body. Let us suppose that to this Phantom of the physical body the etheric body is added; will the Phantom then become visible? Certainly not; for the etheric body is invisible for ordinary sight. Thus the physical body as Phantom, plus etheric body, is still invisible to external physical sense. And the astral body even more so; hence the combination of physical body as Phantom with the etheric and astral bodies is still invisible. And when the Ego is added it would certainly become perceptible inwardly, but not externally visible. Thus, as man came over out of the Saturn, Sun and Moon periods, he was still visible only to a clairvoyant. How did he become visible? But for the occurrence described in the Bible symbolically, and factually in occult science, as the entry of the Lucifer influence, he would not have become visible. What happened through that influence?

Read what is said in *Occult Science*. Out of that path of evolution in which his physical, etheric and astral bodies were still invisible, man was thrown down into denser matter, and was compelled under the influence of Lucifer to take this denser matter into himself. If the Lucifer force had not been introduced into our astral body and Ego, this dense materiality would not have become as visible as it has become. Hence we have to represent man as an invisible being, made visible in matter only through forces which entered into him under the influence of Lucifer. Through this influence external substances and forces are drawn into the domain of the Phantom and permeate it. As when we pour a coloured fluid into a transparent glass, so that the glass looks coloured, so we can imagine that the Lucifer influence poured forces into the human Phantom, with the result that man was adapted for taking in on Earth the requisite substances and forces which make his Form visible. Otherwise his physical body would have remained always invisible.

The alchemists always insisted that the human body really consists of the same substance that constitutes the perfectly transparent, crystal-clear 'Philosopher's Stone'. The physical body is itself entirely transparent, and it is the Lucifer forces in man which have brought him to a non-transparent state and placed him before us so that he is opaque and tangible. Hence you will understand that man has become a being who takes up external substances and forces of the Earth, which are given off again at death, only because Lucifer tempted him, and certain forces were poured into his astral body. It follows that because the Ego entered into connection with the physical, etheric and astral bodies under the influence of Lucifer, man became what he is on earth and otherwise would not have been—the bearer of a visible, earthly organism.

Now let us suppose that at a certain point of time in life the Ego were to go out from a human organism, so that there stood before us physical, etheric and astral bodies, but not the Ego. This is what happened in the case of Jesus of Nazareth in the thirtieth year of His life. The human Ego then left this cohesion of physical, etheric and astral bodies. And into this cohesion the Christ-Being entered at the Baptism in Jordan. We now have the physical, etheric and astral bodies of a man, and the Christ-Being. The Christ-Being had now taken up His abode in a human organism, as otherwise the Ego would have done. What now differentiates this Christ Jesus from all other men on Earth? It is this: that all other men bear within them an Ego that once was overcome by Lucifer's temptation, but Jesus no longer bears an Ego within Him; instead, He bears the Christ-Being. So that from this time, beginning with the Baptism in Jordan, Jesus bears within Himself the residual effects that had come from Lucifer, but with no human Ego to allow any further Luciferic influences to enter his body. A physical body, an etheric body, and astral body—in which the residue of the earlier Luciferic influences was present, but into which no more Luciferic influence could enter—and the Christ-Being: thus was Christ Jesus constituted.

Let us set before us exactly what the Christ is from the Baptism in Jordan until the Mystery of Golgotha: a physical body, an etheric body, and an astral body which makes this physical body together with the etheric body visible because it still contains the residue of the Luciferic influence. Because the Christ-Being had the astral body that Jesus of Nazareth had had from birth to his thirtieth year, the physical body was visible as the bearer of the Christ. Thus from the time of the Baptism in Jordan we have before us a physical body which as such would not be visible on the physical plane; an etheric body which as such would not have been perceptible; the astral body which makes the other two bodies visible and so makes the body of Jesus of Nazareth into a visible body; and, within this organism, the Christ-Being.

We will inscribe firmly in our souls this four-fold nature of Christ Jesus, saying to ourselves: Every person who stands before us on the physical plane consists of physical body, etheric body, astral body and Ego; and this Ego is such that it always works into the astral body up to the hour of death. The Christ-Jesus-Being, however, stands before us as One who had physical body, etheric body and astral body, but no human Ego, so that during the three years up to his death he was not subject to the influences that normally work upon human beings. The only influence came from the Christ-Being.

From this starting-point we will continue to-morrow.

LECTURE VII

Yesterday we saw that in a certain respect the question of Christianity is the question of the Resurrection of Christ Jesus. In particular, we spoke of Paul, the proclaimer of Christianity, who from his knowledge of the essential nature of the Christ-Impulse recognised immediately that after and since the Event of Golgotha, Christ lives. We saw that for Paul, after his experience on the road to Damascus, a powerful, magnificent picture of human evolution opened up.

From this point we went on to build up a picture of what Christ Jesus was directly after the Baptism in Jordan by John. Our next task will be to inquire into the course of events from the Baptism to the Mystery of Golgotha. But if we are to rise to an understanding of the Mystery of Golgotha, we must clear away certain hindrances. From all that has been said concerning the Gospels in the course of years, and also from what has been said already in these few lectures, you will have been able to gather that certain theosophical ideas, which in some quarters are esteemed sufficient, are really not sufficient to answer the question with which we are here concerned.

Before everything else we must take quite seriously what has been said about the three streams of human thought: the stream which has its source in ancient Greece; the stream which comes down from ancient Hebraism, and lastly the stream which found expression in Gautama Buddha half a millennium before our era. We have seen that this Buddha stream, especially as it developed among his followers, is least of all adapted to an understanding of the Mystery of Golgotha. To the modern man, whose consciousness is filled with the intellectual culture of the present day, the stream of thought which finds expression in Buddhism certainly offers something very pleasant. Hardly any other form of thought suits so well the concepts of the present day, in so far as they prefer to remain silent in face of the greatest question that humanity has to grasp—the question of the Resurrection. For with this question the whole evolutionary history of mankind is connected. Now in Buddhist teaching the real being of the Ego, which in the true sense we can call the fourth member of human nature, has been lost. Certainly in these matters one can employ all kinds of interpretations, one can twist them in all sorts of ways, and plenty of people will find fault with what has been said here about Buddhist teaching, but that is not the point. For such things as I have quoted from the heart of Buddhism—for example, the conversation between King Milinda and the Buddhist sage Nagasena—testify clearly that the Ego-nature cannot be spoken of in Buddhism as we must speak of it. For a genuine follower of Buddhism it would indeed be heretical to speak of the Ego-nature as we must represent it. On this very account we must ourselves be clear regarding the Ego-nature.

The human Ego, which in the case of every human being, even of the highest Adept, passes from incarnation to incarnation, is a term which (as we saw yesterday) can be applied to Jesus of Nazareth only from his birth to the Baptism in Jordan. After the baptism, we still have before us the physical body, the etheric body and the astral body of Jesus of Nazareth; but these external human sheaths are now indwelt not by a human Ego but by a Cosmic Being, the Christ-Being. Through years of endeavour we have tried by means of words to bring the Christ-Being nearer to our understanding. As soon as one comprehends the whole nature of Christ Jesus, it is obvious that for Him one must rule out any kind of physical or bodily reincarnation. The expression employed in my mystery drama, *The Soul's Probation*, about Christ having been present once only in a body of flesh, must be taken seriously and quite literally.

Accordingly we must first concern ourselves with the being, the nature, of the ordinary human Ego. The Christ-Jesus-Being was completely independent of the human Ego from the Baptism to the Mystery of Golgotha.

In earlier lectures it was shown that the evolution of the earth was preceded by a Saturn existence, a Sun existence and a Moon existence, and these three planetary embodiments were followed by the fourth, our Earth-embodiment. You know from those lectures that only during the Earth-existence, the fourth of the planetary conditions which were necessary to bring into existence our Earth with all its creatures, could the human Ego enter into connection with human nature. Just as in the Ancient Saturn period we speak of the beginning of the physical body, so in the period of the ancient Sun we speak of the first development of the etheric body, in the Moon period of the first development of the astral body, and only in the Earth period of the unfolding of the Ego. In this way the whole matter is brought cosmically and historically into view. But how is it when we look at the history of peoples?

Through our former studies we know that although the seed-kernel of the Ego was laid down in human beings during the Lemurian time, the possibility of attaining to Ego-consciousness arose only towards the end of the Atlantean period, and that even then this Ego-consciousness was very dim and vague. Indeed, after the Atlantean time, through the various periods of civilisation which preceded the Mystery of Golgotha, the Ego-consciousness was still dull, dream-like, dim. But if you turn your attention to the development of the Hebrew people, it will be clear to you that here the Ego-consciousness found expression in a very unusual way. A kind of Folk-Ego lived in each single member of the ancient Hebrew people; in fact, every member of this people traced his Ego back to his ancestor in the flesh, to Abraham. The Ego of the ancient Hebrew people was still such that we can designate it as a Group-Ego, a Folk-

Group-Ego. Consciousness had not yet penetrated as far as the separate individuality in each man. Why was this so?

Each part of the four-membered human being we now regard as normal developed gradually in the course of the earth's evolution. It was only towards the end of the Atlantean Period that part of the etheric body, which until then had been external to the physical body, was gradually drawn into the body. This led towards the condition now recognised by clairvoyant consciousness as normal, namely that the physical body and the etheric body approximately coincide, and only then was it possible for man to develop his Ego-consciousness Let us slowly and gradually form an impression of the very peculiar way in which this Ego-consciousness meets us in man.

I described yesterday how people speak of the Resurrection when they approach it with all the intellectual preconceptions of the present day. 'If', they say, 'I had to assent to the real Pauline teaching about the Resurrection, I would have to tear up my whole conception of the world.' That is what they say, these up-to-date people who have at their command all the resources of modern intellectualism. To people who speak thus, what must now be said will seem very strange.

But is it not possible that such a person might reflect: 'Yes, if I am to accept the Resurrection, I shall have to tear up all my intellectual concepts. But is that a reason for setting this question aside? Because we cannot understand the Resurrection and have to regard it as a miracle, must we assume that the only way out of this difficulty is to pass it by? Is there no other way?'

The other way is far from easy for a modern man, for he would have to admit to himself: 'Perhaps it is not the fault of the Resurrection that I am unable to understand it. Perhaps the reason is that my intellect is unfitted to understand it.'

So little is this matter taken seriously in our day that we

may say: Modern man is prevented by his pride—and just because he does not suspect that pride could come into it— from admitting that his intellect may be incompetent to fathom this question. For which is more reasonable: to say that I am setting aside something that shatters my intellectual outlook, or to admit that it may be beyond my understanding? Pride, however, forbids this admission.

Of course, an anthroposophist must have trained himself to rise above this kind of pride. It should not be far from the heart of a true anthroposophist to say: 'Perhaps my intellect is not competent to form an opinion about the Resurrection.' But then he has to face another difficulty: he now has to answer the question why the human mind is not adapted to comprehend the greatest fact in human evolution. To answer this question we must go somewhat more closely into the real nature of human understanding. Here I should like to remind you of my Munich lectures, *Wonders of the World,* of which I will now give a résumé as far as we need one.

The elements that go to make up our soul life, our thoughts, feelings and perceptions, are not to be found in our present-day physical body; they penetrate only as far as the etheric body. In order to be clear about this, let us imagine our human nature, in so far as it consists of Ego, astral body and etheric body, enclosed in an ellipse: We will take this dia-

gram to represent schematically what we call our inward life and can experience in our souls; the diagram shows it coming to expression only in the streams and forces of the etheric body. If we experience a thought or perception, it has three lines of action in our soul-nature, as indicated in

the following diagram. Within our soul-nature there is
nothing that is not present in this way. Now if a man's
ordinary earthly consciousness were restricted to soul-
experiences within the confines of the diagram, the experiences would occur, but he would not be conscious of

Soul - experiences

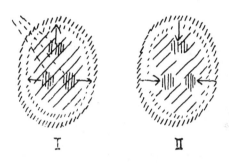

I   II

them; they would remain unconscious. Our soul-experiences
become conscious only through a process which an analogy
will help us to understand. Imagine you are going in a certain
direction, looking straight ahead. Your name is Smith.
While you are going straight ahead you do not see Smith,
yet you are he, you experience him, you are the person
'Smith'. Imagine that someone puts a mirror in front of you.
Now 'Smith' stands before you. What you had previously
experienced you now see; it meets you in the mirror. So it is
with the soul-life of man. A person has an experience, but he
does not become conscious of it without a mirror. The mirror
is the physical body. The perceptions, the thoughts, are
thrown back by the sheath of the physical body. Thereby we
become conscious of them. Hence in the diagram we can
represent the physical body as the enclosing sheath. For us,
as earthly men, the physical body is in truth a reflecting
apparatus.

  If in this way you go more and more deeply into the nature
of the human soul and of human consciousness, it will be

impossible for you to consider as in any way dangerous or significant all those things which are brought forward again and again by materialism in opposition to the spiritual conception of the world. If through any damage to the reflecting apparatus, the soul-experience is no longer perceived by the consciousness, it is absolute nonsense to conclude that the soul-experience itself is bound up with the mirror. If someone breaks a mirror in which you see yourself, he does not break you. You merely disappear from your own field of vision. So it is when the reflecting apparatus for the soul-life, the brain, is disturbed. Perception ceases, but the soul-life itself, in so far as it goes on in the etheric body and the astral body, is not in the least disturbed.

But have we not come to a point when we must consider closely the nature of the physical body? You will agree that without consciousness we could not be conscious of the Ego. In order to make Ego-consciousness our own during life on earth, our physical body, with its brain organisation, has to be a reflecting apparatus. We learn to become conscious of ourselves through our own mirrored reflection. If we had no mirror apparatus, we could not be conscious of our own selves. What is this mirror?

We are shown by occult investigations, which reach back through reading the Akashic record as far as the origin of our earth existence, that in the beginning of Earth-existence this reflecting apparatus, the external physical body, came under Luciferic influence and was changed. Yesterday we saw what this physical body has become for earthly man. It has become something that falls to pieces when he passes through the gate of death. We have said that the body which falls to pieces is not the body which Divine Spirits had prepared through four planetary evolutions so that it should become the physical body on earth. What the Divine Spirits prepared, which yesterday we called the Phantom, belongs to the physical body as a form-body which permeates, and at the same time holds together, the material parts that are woven into our physical body. If no Luciferic influence had intervened, then, at the beginning of his Earth-existence, man would have received this Phantom in full strength together with his physical body. But into the human organisation, in so far as it consists of physical body, etheric body and astral body, the Luciferic influence penetrated, and the consequence was the disorganisation of the Phantom of the physical body. As we shall see, this is symbolically expressed in the Bible as the Fall, together with the fact, related in the Old Testament, that death followed the Fall. Death was indeed the result of the disorganisation of the Phantom of the physical body. The outcome is that, when man goes through the gate of death, he has to see the dissolution of his physical body. This crumbling physical body, lacking the strength of the Phantom, is indeed borne by man from birth to death. The crumbling away goes on all the time, and the decomposition, the death of the physical body, is only the final stage of a continuous process. For if the disintegration of the body—preceded by the disorganisation of the Phantom—is not countered by processes of reconstruction, death finally ensues.

If no Luciferic influence had come in, the destructive and reconstructive forces in the physical body would have remained in balance. But then everything in earthly human nature would have been different; there would, for example, have been no mind incapable of comprehending the Resurrection. For what kind of understanding is it that cannot grasp the Resurrection? It is the kind that is bound up with the decadence of the physical body, and is what it is because the individual has incurred, through the Luciferic influence, the progressive destruction of the Phantom of the physical body. In consequence the human understanding, the human intellect, has become so thin, so threadbare, that it cannot take in the great processes of cosmic evolution. It looks on them as miracles, or says it cannot comprehend them. If the Luciferic influence had not come, and the

upbuilding forces in the human body had held the destructive forces in balance, then the human understanding,
equipped with all that was intended for it, would have seen
into the upbuilding forces, rather as one follows a laboratory
experiment. But our understanding is now such that it
remains on the surface of things and has no insight into the
cosmic depths.

Anyone, therefore, who wishes to characterise these conditions correctly must say: In the beginning of our Earth-
existence, the physical body was prevented by the Luciferic
influence from becoming what it should have become
according to the will of the Powers who worked through
Saturn, Sun and Moon. Instead, it took into itself a destructive process. Since the beginning of the Earth-existence man
has lived in a physical body which is subject to destruction;
a body which cannot adequately counter the destructive
forces with upbuilding forces.

So there is truth in something which appears to the modern
man as such folly: that a hidden connection exists between
what has come to pass through the working of Lucifer, and
death. And now let us look at this working. What was the
effect of this destruction of the real physical body? If we had
the complete physical body, as was intended at the beginning
of the earth-existence, our soul-powers would reflect themselves in quite another way: we should then know in truth
what we are. As things are, we do not know what we are
because the physical body is not given us in its completeness.
We do certainly speak of the nature and being of the human
Ego—but how far does man know the Ego? So problematic
is the Ego that Buddhism can even deny that it goes from
one incarnation to another. So problematic is it that Greece
could fall into the tragic mood which found expression in
those words of the Greek hero: 'Better a beggar in the upper
world than a king in the realm of shades.' So it was that
when a Greek saw the treasured physical body—the body
shaped by the Phantom—given over to destruction, he felt a

sadness in face of the darkening, the fading away, of the Ego, for he felt that it could exist only together with the Ego-consciousness. And when he saw the Form of the physical body falling into decadence, he shuddered at the thought that the Ego would grow dark and dim; this Ego which is reflected by the Form of the physical body. And when we follow human evolution from the beginning of the Earth to the Mystery of Golgotha, we find that the process we have just indicated shows itself in an ever-increasing degree.

In earlier times, for example, no one would have preached the annihilation of the physical body in so radical a fashion as did Gautama Buddha. For such teaching to be given, it was necessary that the decadence of the physical body, its complete annulment as regards its Form, should have become more and more nearly complete, so that the human mind no longer had any idea that the entity which becomes conscious through the physical body—that is, through the Form—can pass over from one incarnation to another. The truth is that man, in the course of the Earth-evolution, lost the Form of the physical body, so that he no longer has what the Divine Beings had intended for him from the beginning of the Earth. This is something he must regain; but it had first to be imparted to him once more. And we cannot comprehend Christianity unless we understand that at the time when the Events of Palestine took place, the human race on earth had reached a stage where the decadence of the physical body was at its peak, and where, because of this, the whole evolution of humanity was threatened with the danger that the Ego-consciousness—the specific achievement of the earth-evolution—would be lost. If this process had continued unchanged, the destructive element would have penetrated ever more deeply into the human bodily organism, and men born after the time when the events of Palestine were due would have had to live with an ever-duller feeling of the Ego. Everything that depends on perfect reflection from the physical body would have become increasingly worn out.

Then came the Mystery of Golgotha; it came as we have characterised it, and through it something happened which is so hard to grasp for an intellect bound up with the physical body only, a body in which the destructive forces preponderate. It came to pass that one man, who was the bearer of the Christ, had gone through such a death that after three days the specifically mortal part of the physical body had to disappear, and out of the grave there rose the body which is the force-bearer of the physical, material parts. The body that was really intended for man by the Rulers of Saturn, Sun and Moon—the pure Phantom of the physical body with all the attributes of the physical body—this it was that rose out of the grave. So was given the possibility of that spiritual genealogy of which we have spoken.

Let us think of the body of Christ that rose out of the grave. Just as from the body of Adam the bodies of earth-men are descended, in so far as these men have the body that crumbles away, even so are the spiritual bodies, the Phantoms for all men, descended from that which rose out of the grave. And it is possible to establish a relationship with Christ through which an earthly human being can bring into his otherwise decaying physical body this Phantom which rose out of the grave of Golgotha. It is possible for man to receive into his organism those forces which then rose from the grave, just as through his physical organism at the beginning of the earth evolution, as a consequence of the Luciferic forces, he received the organism of Adam.

It is this that Paul wishes to say. Just as man, through his place in the stream of physical evolution, inherits the physical body in which the destruction of the Phantom, the force-bearer, is gradually taking place, so from the pure Phantom that rose out of the grave he can inherit what he has lost. He can inherit it, he can clothe himself with it, as he clothed himself with the first Adam; he can become one with it. Thereby he can go through a development by means of which he can climb upwards again, even as before the Mystery of Golgotha he had descended in evolution. In other words, that which had been taken from him through the Luciferic influence can be given back to him through its presence as the Risen Body of Christ. That is what Paul wishes to say.

Now, just as it is very easy, from the standpoint of modern anatomy or physiology, to refute what has been said in this lecture—apparently to refute it—so is it very easy to raise another objection. Some such question as this might be asked: If indeed Paul really believed that a spiritual body had risen, what has this spiritual body which had risen out of the grave to do with what every man now bears in himself? This is not hard to understand: we need only consider the analogy offered by the coming into existence of a human individual. As physical human being he begins from a single cell; a physical body consists entirely of cells which are all children of the original cell; all cells which compose a human body are traceable to the original cell. Now imagine that, through what we may call a mystical Christological process, man acquires a body quite other than the one he has gradually acquired in his downward evolution. Then think of each of these new bodies as having an intimate connection with the pure Phantom that rose from the grave, somewhat as the human cells of the physical body are connected with the original cell. That is, we must think of the Phantom as multiplying itself, as does the cell which gives rise to the physical body. So, in the evolution which follows the Event of Golgotha, every man can inwardly acquire something which is spiritually descended from the Phantom which rose from the grave, just as—to echo Paul—the ordinary body which falls into dissolution is descended from Adam.

Of course it is an insult to the human intellect, which thinks so arrogantly of itself at the present time, when one says that a process similar to the multiplication of the cell, which if need be can be seen, takes place in the invisible. This outcome of the Mystery of Golgotha, however, is an occult fact. To someone who contemplates evolution with occult sight it is apparent that the spiritual cell, the body which overcame death, the body of Christ Jesus, has risen from the grave and in the course of time imparts itself to anyone who enters into the corresponding relationship with the Christ. To anyone resolved to deny supersensible happenings altogether, this statement will naturally seem absurd. But to anyone who grants the supersensible, the event with which we are here concerned must be presented in the way described. The Phantom which rose from the grave communicates itself to those who make themselves fitted for it. This, then, is a fact that everyone who grants the supersensible can understand.

If we can inscribe upon our souls what is in very truth the Pauline teaching, we come to regard the Mystery of Golgotha as a reality that took place and had to take place in the evolution of the earth; for it signifies literally the rescue of the human Ego. We have seen that if the process of evolution had continued along the path it had followed up to the time of the Events of Palestine, the Ego-consciousness could not have been developed; it would not only have failed to advance, but would have gone down ever further into darkness. But the path turned upwards, and will continue to ascend in proportion as men find their relation to the Christ-Being.

Now we can understand Buddhism very well. About five hundred years before the Events of Palestine, a truth was proclaimed: 'Everything that envelops a man as his physical body and makes him a being incarnated in the flesh—all this must be looked upon as worthless; it is fundamentally a left-over from the past and must be cast off.' Certainly up to that time conditions were such that humanity would have had to set its course towards this philosophy of life, if nothing else had intervened. But there came the Event of Golgotha, an Event which completely restored the lost principles of human evolution. In so far as man takes into himself the incorruptible body we spoke of yesterday, and have brought before our souls in closer detail today, if he clothes himself with this incorruptible body, he will become more and more clearly aware of his Ego-consciousness, and of that part of his nature which journeys on from one incarnation to another.

That which came into the world with Christianity must therefore not be regarded merely as a new teaching—this must be specially emphasised—and not as a new theory, but as something real, something factual. Hence when people insist that everything Christ taught had been known previously, this signifies nothing for a real understanding of Christianity. The important thing is not what Christ taught, but what he gave: his Body. For the Body that rose from the grave of Golgotha had never before entered into human evolution. Never before had there been present on earth, through the death of a man, that which came to be present as the Risen Body of Christ Jesus. Previously, after men had passed through the gate of death, and had gone through the period between death and a new birth, they had brought to earth with them the defective Phantom, given over to deterioration. No one had ever caused a perfect Phantom to arise.

Here we can refer to the Initiates and Adepts. They always had to receive initiation outside their physical bodies, by overcoming their physical bodies, but this overcoming never went as far as a resuscitation of the physical Phantom. No pre-Christian initiations went farther than the outermost limits of the physical body; they did not touch the forces of the physical body, except in so far as the inner organism impinges in a general way on the outer. No one, having gone through death, had ever overcome death as a human Phantom. Similar things had certainly occurred, but never this—that a man had gone through a complete human death and that the complete Phantom had then gained victory over death. Just as it is true that only this Phantom can give rise to a complete humanity in the course of human evolution, so is it true that this Phantom took its beginning from the grave of Golgotha.

That is the important fact in Christian evolution. Hence the commentators are not at fault when they say again and again that the teaching of Christ Jesus has been transformed into a teaching about Christ Jesus. It had to be so. For the important thing is not what Christ Jesus taught, but what He gave to humanity. His Resurrection is the coming to birth of a new member of human nature—an incorruptible body. But for this to happen, this rescue of the human Phantom through death, two things were necessary. It was necessary, first, that the Being of Christ Jesus should be such as we have described it—constituted of physical body, etheric body, and astral body, and—instead of a human ego—the Christ-Being. Secondly, it was necessary that the Christ-Being should have resolved to descend into a human body, to incarnate in a human body of flesh. For if we are to contemplate the Christ-Being in the right light, we must seek Him in the time before the beginning of man on earth. The Christ-Being was of course existent at that time. He did not enter into the course of human evolution; He dwelt in the spiritual world. Humanity continued along its ever-decreasing path. At a point in time when the crisis of human evolution had been reached, the Christ-Being incorporated Himself in the body of a man. That is the greatest sacrifice that could have been brought to the earth-evolution by the Christ-Being. And the second thing we must learn to understand is wherein this sacrifice consisted. Yesterday we dealt with one part of the question concerning the nature of Christ, confining our study to the time after the Baptism by John in Jordan. We must now go on to ask: What is the significance of the fact that at the Baptism the Christ-Being descended into a body of flesh, and how did death come about in the Mystery of Golgotha?

This question will occupy us in the coming days.

LECTURE VIII

Yesterday we indicated that it was now necessary to answer the question: What really happened to that Being whom we designate as Christ Jesus from the Baptism by John in Jordan to the Mystery of Golgotha? To answer this question as far as possible, we must recall briefly what we know from former lectures concerning the life of Jesus of Nazareth, who in his thirtieth year became the bearer of the Christ. The essential points are given in my recently published book, *The Spiritual Guidance of Mankind.*

We know that in Palestine, at the time which concerns us, not one but two Jesus-children were born, one of them from the Solomon line of the House of David. This is the Jesus child of whom the Matthew Gospel speaks. The peculiar contradiction between the beginnings of the Matthew and the Luke Gospels derives from the fact that the writer of the Matthew Gospel was concerned with one of the Jesus-children, the one born from the Solomon line. Then, at almost but not quite the same time, another Jesus-child was born, from the Nathan line of the House of David.

The important thing is to understand clearly what kind of beings these two children were. Occult investigation shows that the individuality who was in the Solomon Jesus-child was none other than Zarathustra. After Zarathustra's most important mission, of which we have spoken in connection with the ancient Persian civilisation, he had been incarnated again and again; lastly during the Babylonian-Chaldaic civilisation, and now as the Solomon Jesus-child. This Zarathustra individuality, with all the great and powerful inner forces which in the nature of things he had brought over from earlier incarnations, had to incarnate in a body descended from the Solomon side of the House of David; a body adapted for working up and further developing the great faculties of Zarathustra, in the way that human faculties, when they are already at a very high level, can be brought further on, in so far as they belong to the being who is going from incarnation to incarnation. We are concerned therefore with a human body which did not wait until later years to work on these faculties, but could do so in a youthful, child-like and yet powerful organism. Hence we see the Zarathustra-individuality growing up in such a way that the faculties of the child developed comparatively early. The child soon showed an extent of knowledge which would normally have been impossible at his age.

One fact, however, we must keep firmly in mind: the Solomon Jesus-child, although the incarnation of so lofty an individuality, was only a highly developed man. Hence he was encumbered—as even the most highly developed man must be—with certain liabilities to error and moral difficulties, though not exactly vices or sins. Then we know that in his twelfth year the individuality of Zarathustra, by an occult process known to everyone who has made himself conversant with such facts, forsook the body of the Solomon Jesus-child and went over into the body of the Nathan Jesus-child. Now the body of this Nathan Jesus-child—or, better, his three-fold bodily organisation physical body, etheric body, astral body—was formed in a quite special manner. In fact, this body was such that the child showed capacities exactly contrary to those of the Solomon Jesus-child. Whereas the latter was remarkable because of his great gifts in relation to things one can learn externally, it might almost be said that in this respect the Nathan Jesus-child was untalented. You will understand that saying this implies not the slightest deprecation. The Nathan Jesus-child was not in a position to familiarise himself with the products of human culture on earth. By contrast, the remarkable fact is that he could speak as soon as he was born. A faculty which belongs more to the physical body was thus present in him from his birth. But—according to a good tradition which can be occultly confirmed—the language he spoke could be understood by his Mother only. The child's most strongly marked characteristics were qualities of the heart. He had an immense capacity for love and a disposition capable of immense self-sacrifice. And the remarkable thing is that from the first days of his life his mere presence, or his touch, had beneficent effects—magnetic effects, one might perhaps call them nowadays. Thus all the qualities of heart were manifest in this child, enhanced to such a degree that they could have a beneficent magnetic influence on his environment.

We know also that active in the astral body of this child were the forces which had once been acquired by that Bodhisattva who became Gautama Buddha. We know indeed—and in this respect the oriental tradition is absolutely correct, for it can be confirmed by occult science—that the Bodhisattva, who on becoming Buddha five centuries before our era no longer needed to incarnate further on earth, worked from the spiritual world upon all those who devoted themselves to his teachings. It is characteristic of such an individuality, who rises to heights from which he need no longer incarnate in a body of flesh, that he can then take part in the affairs and destiny of our earth existence from out of the spiritual worlds. This can happen in the most manifold ways. In fact, the Bodhisattva who went through his last incarnation on the earth as Gautama Buddha has taken an essential part in the further evolution of humanity. Our human spiritual world stands continually in connection with all the rest of the spiritual world. The human being not only eats and drinks and so takes into himself the substance of the physical earth; he continually receives soul-spiritual nourishment from the spiritual world. In the most varied ways forces continually flow into physical earthly-existence from out of the spiritual world. Such an in-flow of the forces which Buddha had gained for himself came into the wider stream of humanity through the fact that the Buddha forces permeated the astral body of the Nathan Jesus-child. We know, too, from earlier lectures that the words we still have to-day as a Christmas message—'The Divine reveals itself from the heights, and on earth peace will spread in the hearts of men of good will!'—originate in essence from the influence which flowed down into human evolution through the immersion of the Buddha powers in the astral body of the Nathan Jesus-child.

Thus we see the Buddha forces working further in the stream of earth-existence which took its start from the Events of Palestine. And it is interesting that precisely the researches made by western occultism in quite recent years have led to the recognition of a very important connection between European civilisation and the Buddha forces. For a long time these Buddha forces have been working from the spiritual worlds, particularly upon everything in Western civilisation which is unthinkable without the specific influence of Christianity. All those philosophical streams which have developed during recent centuries up to the nineteenth century, in so far as they are Western spiritual currents, are permeated by the Christ-Impulse, but the Buddha has always been working into them from out of the spiritual worlds. Hence the most important thing that European humanity can receive from Buddha today does not depend on the handing down of the teaching that Buddha gave to men about 500 years before the Christian era, but on what he has become since that time. For he has not remained at a standstill; he has progressed; and it is through this progress, as a spiritual being in the spiritual worlds, that he has in the highest sense been able to take part in the further evolution of Western civilisation. The outcome of our own occult investigation harmonises in a wonderful way with much that had been known previously, before this important influence could be investigated again. For we know that the same individuality who appeared as Gautama

Buddha in the East had previously worked in the West, and that certain legends and traditions connected with the name of Buddha or Wotan have to do with this same individuality, just as Buddhism has with Gautama Buddha in the East; hence the same field of action in human evolution which had been prepared earlier by the same individuality has again been occupied in a certain sense. Thus are interlaced the ways taken by the spiritual currents within the evolution of humanity.

To-day the most important thing for us is to establish that in the astral body of the Jesus-child described by Luke we have the Buddha forces at work. And when this Nathan Jesus-child was twelve years old, the Zarathustra individuality passed over into his three-fold being.

Why is it, then, that this Jesus-child had the remarkable qualities we have just characterised? It was because he was not a human individuality like every other, but in a certain respect quite different, and in order to understand him we must go back to the ancient Lemurian time in which, strictly speaking, the Earth-evolution of man took its start. We must clearly understand that everything before the Lemurian time was really only a repetition of the Saturn, Sun and Moon periods. Only in the Lemurian time was the first germ-condition laid down in man as a potentiality, so that during the Earth-evolution he could receive the fourth member of his being, the Ego. We can say the extension of mankind over the Earth—a subject dealt with more precisely in the *Outline of Occult Science*—is to be traced to certain human ancestors in the Lemurian period, the period with which our present Earth took its start.

It is only after a certain point of time in this Lemurian period that we can speak correctly, in a modern sense, of the human race. Before this, those Egos who have since continued to incarnate were not present in men on Earth. They were not yet separate from the substance of that Hierarchy which had first brought the human Ego into being: the Hierarchy of the Spirits of Form. We can now picture to ourselves—occult research shows this—that part of the substance of the Spirits of Form entered into the incarnations of men for the building up of the human Ego. But when in due time man was given over to his physical incarnations on the Earth, something was held back. A certain Ego substance was not brought into the stream of physical incarnations. If we were to represent the stream of physical human incarnations, beginning with him whom the Bible calls 'Adam', the progenitor of the human race, we should have to draw a genealogical tree with widespreading branches. Instead, let us simply imagine that the substance poured down from the Spirits of Form now flows onward, but that something was held back: an Ego that was now protected from entering into physical incarnations. Instead, this Ego preserved the form, the substantiality, which man had had before proceeding to his first earthly incarnation. This Ego lived on collaterally with the rest of humanity, and at the time of which we are now speaking, when the Event of Palestine was to take place, it was still in the same condition, if we wish to speak according to the Bible, as was the Ego of Adam before his first embodiment in flesh.

In examining what occult science knows about this Ego—which naturally for modern man is something extremely foolish—we see that this Ego, which was, as it were held back 'in reserve', was given into the care of the Holy Mysteries through Atlantean and post-Atlantean times. It was preserved in an important Mystery centre, as in a tabernacle, and because of this it had quite special characteristics; it was untouched by everything that a human Ego could have learnt on Earth. It was therefore untouched by any Luciferic and Ahrimanic influences; it was indeed something we can think of, in contrast to other human Egos, as an empty sphere, still completely virginal with regard to all earth experiences—a nothing, a negative, in this respect. Hence it seemed as though the Nathan-child, described in the Luke Gospel, really had no Ego; as though he consisted only of physical, etheric and astral body. And it is quite adequate if at first we say that an Ego, developed as Egos had developed in Atlantean and post-Atlantean times, was not there at all in the Luke Jesus-child.

We speak in the true sense of the words when we say that in the Matthew Jesus-child we have to do with a completely human being; whereas in the Nathan Jesus-child of the Luke Gospel we have to do with a physical, an etheric and an astral body which are inter-related in the harmonious unity that belonged to man when he emerged from the Saturn, Sun and Moon evolutions. Hence this Jesus-child, as the Akashic Record tells us, was untalented for all that human culture had developed. He could not receive it because he had never been among it. External abilities and adaptations to existence are the outcome of certain experiences in earlier incarnations. Anyone who had never shared in such experiences would show himself without talent for all that men have accomplished during the earth-evolution. If the Nathan Jesus-child had been born in our time, he would have been totally ungifted for learning to write, since in Adamic times writing was unknown. By contrast, the Luke Jesus-child revealed in a high degree the qualities he had brought with him—qualities that had not fallen into decadence through the Luciferic influence. Even more interesting is the remarkable language he spoke.

Here we must bring to mind something I mentioned in *The Spiritual Guidance of Mankind*: that the languages which are now spread over the earth took their rise comparatively late in evolution: they were preceded by what can truly be called a primal human language. It is the disuniting spirits of the Luciferic and Ahrimanic world who have made many languages out of the primal language. The primal language is lost, and can be spoken to-day by nobody with an Ego which in the course of earth-evolution has passed from incarnation to incarnation. This Jesus-child, who had not gone through human incarnations, acquired from the starting-point of human evolution the faculty of speaking, not this or that language, but a language of which we can rightly say that it was not comprehensible to those around him. But, because of the inner qualities of heart that lived in it, it was understood by his Mother's heart. This points to a phenomenon of immense significance in the case of the Luke Jesus-child.

We have seen that when this Luke Jesus-child was born, he was provided with everything that had not been influenced by the Lucifer-Ahrimanic forces. He did not possess an Ego that had been through a series of incarnations; therefore nothing had to be discarded when, in his twelfth year, the individuality of Zarathustra passed over from the Solomon Jesus-child into the Nathan Jesus-child. I have already said that the human element which had remained behind, and up to this time had developed in the Mysteries by the side of the rest of humanity, was born for the first time in the Palestine period as the Nathan Jesus-child. There was a transference from a Mystery centre in Western Asia, where this human kernel had been preserved, into the body of the Nathan Jesus-child. This child grew on, and in his twelfth year the individuality of Zarathustra passed into him. We know also that this passing over is intimated in the scene of the twelve-year-old Jesus in the Temple. It was quite natural that the parents of the Nathan Jesus-child, who were accustomed to regard him in the light we have described, should find a remarkable change when they discovered him in the Temple after he had been lost. For that was the moment when Zarathustra passed over into this twelve-year-old child. From the twelfth to the thirtieth year, therefore, we have to do with the individuality of Zarathustra in the Luke Jesus-child.

Now in the Luke Gospel we have a remarkable expression which indicates something that can be made clear only by occult investigation. You know that in the Luke Gospel, after the description of the scene with the twelve-year-old Jesus in the Temple, there is a passage: 'And Jesus increased in wisdom and stature, and in favour with God and man'. (Luke II:52). In truth this passage stands as follows when we restore the text of the Gospels from the Akashic record: The twelve-year-old child increased in everything wherein an astral body can increase, i.e., in wisdom; in everything wherein an etheric body can increase, i.e. in all the qualities of kindliness, goodness, etc; and in everything wherein a physical body can increase, i.e., in all that pours itself into external beauty of form. In this passage, therefore, a special indication is given that the Jesus-child, not having gone from incarnation to incarnation, had up to his twelfth year remained untouched, and could not be touched in his individuality, by the Luciferic and Ahrimanic forces. The Luke Gospel intimates this again by tracing the sequence of generations back through Adam to God, thus indicating that the substance in question was uninfluenced by all that had taken place in human evolution.

So this Jesus-child lived on, increasing in all that was possible for a three-fold organism not touched by the contamination which has affected the three-fold bodies of other men. And this enabled the individuality of Zarathustra, from the twelfth to the thirtieth year of life, to pour into this three-fold human being all that could come from the heights to which he himself had previously attained. Hence we form a correct idea of Jesus of Nazareth, up to the thirtieth year of his life, when we think of him as a lofty human individuality, for whose coming into existence the greatest possible preparations had been made.

But we must now be clear about one thing if we want to understand how the fruits of a development we go through in our bodies are of benefit to the individuality. Our bodies enable our individuality to absorb the fruits of our life for its future evolution. When in death we forsake our bodies, we do not usually leave in them what we have achieved and gained for ourselves as individuals. Later on we shall see under what special conditions something may remain in the bodies; but it is not the rule that the individuality should leave behind in his bodies whatever he has won for himself. When Zarathustra forsook the threefold bodily being of Jesus of Nazareth in the thirtieth year, he left behind the three bodies, physical, etheric and astral. But all that he had been able to gain through these instruments went into the individuality of Zarathustra and lived on further with him, to his benefit. Something however, was gained by the three-fold bodily organism of Jesus of Nazareth. His human nature, still free, as it always had been, from Luciferic and Ahrimanic influences, was conjoined for a period with the individuality who had unequalled insight into the spirituality of the cosmos.

Think what this Zarathustra had experienced! While he was founding the ancient Persian civilisation and looking up to the great Sun Spirit, he was even then gazing out into the cosmic realms of the spiritual. Through successive incarnations his development went on. When the innermost part of human nature, together with the most intensive powers of sympathy and love, had become manifest through the unsullied human substance which had been preserved until the birth of the Nathan Jesus, and when the astral body had permeated itself with the forces of Gautama Buddha, there was present in this child what we may call the most intimate inwardness of man. And then into this bodily nature there entered the individuality who above all others had seen most clearly and deeply into the spirituality of the Macro-cosm. By this means the bodily instrument, the entire organism, of the Nathan Jesus was so transformed that it could be the vehicle capable of receiving into itself the Christ-extract of the Macrocosm. If this bodily nature had not been permeated by the Zarathustra-Individuality up to the thirtieth year, the eyes would not have been able to endure the substance of the Christ from the thirtieth year up to the Mystery of Golgotha; the hands would not have been capable of being permeated with the substance of the Christ in the thirtieth year. To be able to receive the Christ, this bodily nature had to be prepared, expanded, through the individuality of Zarathustra. Thus in Jesus of Nazareth, as he was at the moment when Zarathustra took leave of him and the Christ-Individuality entered into him, we have to do neither with an adept, nor with anything like a higher human being. For an adept is an adept because he has a highly developed individuality, and it was just this that had passed out of the threefold bodily nature of Jesus of Nazareth. We have simply the bodily nature so prepared through the indwelling of Zarathustra that it could take into itself the Christ-Individuality. But now, through the union of the Christ-Individuality with this bodily nature, by necessity the following consequence came about.

During these three years, from the Baptism by John in Jordan onwards to the Mystery of Golgotha, the development of the physical body, the etheric body and the astral body was quite different from the bodily development of other human beings. Since the Nathan Jesus had received no influence from the Luciferic and Ahrimanic powers, the possibility was given that, from the Baptism in Jordan onwards—now that there was in Jesus of Nazareth no human Ego, but solely the Christ Individuality—everything which is normally at work in a human organism was not developed.

We said yesterday that the human Phantom, the primal form which draws into itself the material elements that fill out the physical body and are laid aside at death, had degenerated in the course of time up to the Mystery of Golgotha. At the beginning of human evolution it was intended that the Phantom should remain untouched by the material elements that man takes for his nutrition from the animal, plant and mineral kingdoms. But it did not remain untouched. For the Luciferic influence brought about a close connection between the Phantom and the forces which man absorbs through his earthly evolution; a connection particularly with the ashy constituents. The result was that the Phantom, while continuing to accompany man during his further evolution, was strongly drawn to these ashy constituents, and instead of adhering to the etheric body, it attached itself to these products of disintegration. But where the Luciferic influences had been kept away, as they were from the Nathan Jesus, no force of attraction arose between the Phantom and the material elements that had been taken into the bodily organism. Throughout the three years from the Baptism up to the Mystery of Golgotha, the Phantom remained untouched by these elements.

In occult terms we can say: The human Phantom, according to its intended development through the Saturn, Sun and Moon periods, should not have been attracted to the ashy constituents but only to the dissolving salt constituents, so that it would have taken the path of volatilisation in so far as the salt constituents dissolved. In an occult sense one can say that it would have dissolved and passed over, not into the earth but into the volatile constituents. The remarkable fact is that with the Baptism in Jordan and the entry of the Christ Individuality into the body of the Nathan Jesus, all connection of the Phantom with the ashy constituents was wiped out; only the connection with the salt constituents remained.

This is alluded to in the passage where Christ Jesus wishes to explain to his first-chosen disciples: 'Through the way in which you feel yourselves united with the Christ Being, a certain possibility for the future evolution of humanity will come about. It will be possible for the one body risen from the grave—the spiritual body—to pass over into men'. That is what Christ wished to say when he used the phrase, 'You are the salt of the earth'. All these words we find in the Gospels, reminding us of the terminology and craft language of the later alchemists, the later occultism, have the deepest imaginable significance. And in fact this significance was well known to the mediaeval and later alchemists—not to the charlatans mentioned in the history books—and not one of them spoke of these connections without feeling in his heart a connection with Christ.

Thus it followed that when Christ Jesus was crucified, when his body was nailed to the Cross—you will notice that here I use the exact words of the Gospel, for they are confirmed by true occult research—when this body of Jesus of Nazareth was fastened to the Cross, the Phantom was perfectly intact; it existed in a spiritual bodily form, visible only to supersensible sight, and was much more loosely connected with the body's material content of earth-elements than has ever happened with any other human being. In every other human being a connection of the Phantom with these elements has occurred, and it is this that holds them together. In the case of Christ Jesus it was quite different. The ordinary law of inertia sees to it that certain material portions of a human body hold together after death in the form man has given them, until after some time they crumble away, so that hardly anything of them is visible. So it was with the material portions of the body of Christ Jesus. When the body was taken down from the Cross, the parts were still coherent, but they had no connection with the Phantom; the Phantom was completely free of them. When the body became permeated with certain substances, which in this case worked quite differently from the way in which they affect any other body that is embalmed, it came to pass that after the burial the material parts quickly volatilised and passed over into the elements. Hence the disciples who looked into the grave found the linen cloths in which the body had been wrapped, but the Phantom, on which the evolution of the Ego depends, had risen from the grave. It is not surprising that Mary of Magdala, who had known only the earlier Phantom when it was permeated by earthly elements, did not recognise the same form in the Phantom, now freed from terrestrial gravity, when she saw it clairvoyantly. It seemed to her different.

Moreover we must clearly understand that it was only through the power of the companionship of the disciples with the Christ that all the disciples, and all those persons of whom the same is told, could see the Risen One, for He appeared to them in the spiritual body, the body of which Paul says that it increases as a grain of seed and passes over into all people. Paul himself is convinced that it was not a body permeated by the earthly elements which had appeared to the other apostles, but that the same which had appeared to him had also appeared to them, as he says in the following passage:

> For I have delivered unto you as of first importance what I also received, that Christ died for our sins in accordance with the scriptures, that He was buried, that he was raised on the third day in accordance with the scriptures; and that he appeared to Cephas, then to the twelve. Then he appeared to more than five hundred brethren at one time, most of whom are still alive, though some have fallen asleep. Then He appeared to James, then to all the apostles. Last of all, as to one untimely born, he appeared also to me. (I Corinthians XV: 3–8.)

But what was it that convinced Paul? In a certain sense Paul was an Initiate before the Event of Damascus. His Initiation had combined the ancient Hebrew principle and the Greek principle. He knew that an Initiate became, in his etheric body, independent of the physical body, and could appear in the purest form of his etheric body to those who were capable of seeing it. If Paul had had the vision of a pure etheric body, independent of a physical body, he would have spoken differently. He would have said that he had seen someone who had been initiated and would be living on further in the course of earth-evolution, independently of the physical body. He would not have found this particularly surprising. What Paul experienced on the road to Damascus could not have been that. He had experienced something which he knew could be experienced only when the Scriptures were fulfilled; when a perfect human Phantom, a human body risen from the grave in a supersensible form, would appear in the spiritual atmosphere of the earth. And that is what he saw! That is what appeared to him on the road to Damascus and left him with the conviction: 'He was there—He is risen! For what is there could come only from Him: it is the Phantom which can be seen by all human individualities who seek to relate themselves to the Christ.' This is what convinced him that Christ was already there; that he would not come first in the future, but was actually present there in a physical body, and that this physical body had rescued the primal form of the human physical body for the salvation of all men.

That this deed could be accomplished only through the greatest unfolding of divine love, and in what sense it was an act of love, and then in what sense the word 'salvation' is to be understood in the further evolution of humanity—this will be our subject to-morrow.

LECTURE IX

The lectures given so far have led essentially to two questions. One relates to the objective event connected with the name, Christ Jesus; to the nature of that impulse which as the Christ-Impulse entered into human evolution. The other question is: how can an individual establish his connection with the Christ-Impulse? In other words, how can the Christ-Impulse become effective for the individual? The answers to these two questions are of course interrelated. For we have seen that the Christ-Event is an objective fact of human Earth-evolution, and that something real, something actual, comes forth to meet us in the Resurrection. With Christ there rose out of the grave a kind of seed-kernel for the reconstruction of our human Phantom. And it is possible for this seed-kernel to incorporate itself in those individuals who find a connection with the Christ-Impulse.

That is the objective side of the relationship of the individual to the Christ-Impulse. To-day we wish to add the subjective side. We will try to find an answer to the question: 'How does the individual now find it possible gradually to take into himself that which comes forth through the Resurrection of Christ?'

To answer this question, we must first distinguish between two things. When Christianity entered into the world as a religion, it was not merely a religion for those who wished to approach Christ by one or other of the spiritual paths. It was to be a religion which all men could accept and make their own. A special occult or esoteric development was not necessary for finding the way to Christ. We must therefore fix our attention first on that path to Christ, the exoteric path, which every soul, every heart, can find in the course of time. We must then distinguish this path from the esoteric path which right up to our own time has revealed itself to the soul who desired to seek the Christ by gaining access to occult powers. We must distinguish between the path of the physical plane and the path of the supersensible worlds.

In hardly any other century has there been such obscurity concerning the outward, exoteric way to Christ as in the nineteenth. And this obscurity increased during the second half of the century. More and more men came to lose the knowledge of the way to Christ. Those imbued with the thought of to-day no longer form the right concepts, such concepts for example as souls even in the eighteenth century formed on their way to the Christ-Impulse. Even the first half of the nineteenth century was illumined by a certain possibility of finding the Christ-Impulse as something real. But for the most part in the nineteenth century this path to Christ was lost to men. And we can understand this when we realise that we are standing at the beginning of a new path to Christ. We have often spoken of the new way now opening for souls through a renewal of the Christ-Event. In human evolution it always happens that a kind of low point must be reached in any trend before a new light comes in once more. The turning away from the spiritual worlds during the nineteenth century was only natural in face of the fact that in the twentieth century a quite new epoch for the spiritual life of men must begin, in the special sense we have often mentioned.

To those who have come to know something of Spiritual Science, our Movement often appears to be something quite new. If, however, we look away from the enrichment that spiritual endeavours in the West have experienced recently through the inflow of the concepts of reincarnation and karma, bound up with the whole teaching of repeated earth lives and its significance for human evolution, we must say that, in other respects, ways into the spiritual world, similar to our theosophical way, are by no means new in Western history. Anyone, however, who tries to rise into the spiritual world along the present path of Theosophy will find himself somewhat estranged from the manner in which Theosophy was cultivated in the eighteenth century. At that time in this neighbourhood (Baden), and especially in Württemberg, much Theosophy was studied, but everywhere an illuminated view of the teaching concerning repeated earth lives was lacking, and thereby a cloud was cast over the whole field of theosophical work. For those who could look deeply into occult connections, and particularly into the connection of the world with the Christ-Impulse, what they saw was over-shadowed for this reason. But within the whole horizon of Christian philosophy and Christian life, something like theosophical endeavours arose continually. This striving towards Theosophy was active everywhere, even in the outward, exoteric paths of men who could go no further than sharing externally in the life of some congregation, Christian or otherwise.

How theosophical endeavours penetrated Christian en-deavours is shown by figures such as Bengel and Oetinger, who worked in Württemberg, men who in their whole way of thinking—if we remember that they lacked the idea of reincarnation—reached all that man can reach of higher views concerning evolution, in so far as they had made the Christ-Impulse their own. The ground-roots of theosophical life have always existed. Hence there is much that is correct in a treatise on theosophical subjects written by Oetinger in the eighteenth century. In the preface to a book on Oetinger's work, published in 1847, Rothe, who taught in Heidelberg University, wrote:

What Theosophy really wants is often difficult to recog-nise in the case of the older theosophists . . . but it is none the less clear that Theosophy, as far as it has gone to-day, can claim no scientific status and therefore cannot extend its influence more widely. It would be very hasty to conclude that Theosophy is only an ephemeral phenomenon, and entirely unjustifiable from a scientific standpoint. History already testifies loudly enough to the contrary. It tells us how this enigmatic phenomenon has never been able to accomplish anything, and yet, unnoticed, it is continually breaking through afresh, held together in its most varied forms by the chain of a never-dying tradition.

Now we must remember that the man who wrote this learnt about Theosophy only in the forties of the nineteenth century, as it had come over from many theosophists of the eighteenth. What came over was certainly not clothed in the forms of our scientific thought. It was therefore difficult to believe that the Theosophy of that time could affect wider circles. Apart from this, such a voice, coming to us out of the forties of the nineteenth century, must appear significant when it says:

The main thing is that once Theosophy has become a real science, and has thus clearly yielded definite results, these will gradually become matters of general and even popular conviction, and will be regarded as accepted truths by people who could not follow the paths by which they were discovered and by which alone they could be discovered.

After this, certainly, comes a pessimistic paragraph with which, in its bearing on Theosophy, we cannot now agree. For anyone familiar with the present form of spiritual-scientific endeavours will be convinced that this Theosophy, in the form in which it desires to work, can become popular in the widest circles. Even such a paragraph may therefore inspire us with courage when we read further:

Still, this rests in the lap of the future, and there we will not encroach: for the present we will gratefully rejoice in what our valued Oetinger has so beautifully set forth, and

which may certainly count upon a sympathetic reception
in a wide circle.

Thus we see that Theosophy was a pious hope of those
who came to know something of the old Theosophy that was
handed down from the eighteenth century.

After that time the stream of theosophical life was buried
under the materialistic trends of the nineteenth century.
Only through what we may now accept as the dawn of a
new age do we again approach the true spiritual life, and
now in a form which can be so scientific that in principle
every heart and every soul can understand it. During the
nineteenth century there was a complete loss of understanding for something that the theosophists of the eighteenth
century still fully possessed; they called it *Zentralsinn* (inner
light). Oetinger, who worked in Murrhard, near Karlsruhe,
was for a time the pupil of a quite simple man in Thuringia,
named Voelker, whose pupils knew that he possessed what
was called 'inner light'. What in those days was this 'inner
light'? It was none other than that which now arises in every
man when earnestly and with iron energy he works through
the content of my book, *Knowledge of the Higher Worlds*. It
was fundamentally nothing else that this simple man of
Thuringia possessed. What he brought into existence—for his
time a very interesting Theosophy—was the teaching which
influenced Oetinger. It is difficult for a man of the present
day to reconcile himself to the knowledge that a deepening of
Theosophy occurred so recently, and gave rise to a rich
literature, buried though this is in libraries and among
antiquarians.

Something else is equally difficult for a man of to-day: to
accept the Christ-Event as first of all an objective fact. How
much discussion of this matter there was in the nineteenth
century! It is impossible in a short course to indicate even in
outline how many and diverse are the views of the nineteenth
century concerning Christ Jesus. And anyone who takes the

trouble to inquire further into opinions concerning Christ Jesus, whether those of theologians or of laymen, will encounter some very real difficulties, if the views of the nineteenth century on this question are considered in relation to the times in which better traditions still prevailed. In the nineteenth century it even became possible for persons to be regarded as great theologians when they were far removed from any acceptance of an objective Christ who entered into and worked in the history of the world. And here we come to the question: What relationship to the Christ can be found by an individual who takes no esoteric path, but remains entirely in the field of the exoteric?

So long as we keep to the standpoint of those nineteenth-century theologians who held that human evolution can take its course purely in the inner being of man, and has nothing to do with the external world of the Macrocosm, we cannot reach an objective appreciation of Christ Jesus; we come to all kinds of grotesque ideas, but never to a relationship with the Christ-Event. For anyone who believes that he can reach the highest human ideal compatible with Earth-evolution merely by an inner soul-path, through a kind of self-redemption, a relationship with the objective Christ is impossible. We may also say that wherever the redemption of man is thought of as a matter for psychology to deal with, there is no relationship to the Christ. Anyone who penetrates further into cosmic mysteries soon finds that when a man believes that he can attain his highest ideal of Earth-existence solely through himself, only through his own inner development, he cuts off altogether his connection with the Macrocosm. Such a person believes that he has the Macrocosm *before* him as a kind of Nature, and that his inner soul-development, *side by side* with the Macrocosm, is something running parallel with it. But a connection between the two he cannot find. This is just what is so terribly grotesque in the evolution of the nineteenth century. The connection that should exist between Microcosm and Macrocosm, has been torn asunder. If this had not happened, we should not have seen all those misunderstandings that have arisen over the terms 'theoretical materialism' on the one hand and 'abstract idealism' on the other. Just consider—the sundering of Microcosm and Macrocosm has led men who care little for the inner life of the soul to assign it, as well as the external life of the body, to the Macrocosm, thus making everything subject to material processes. Others, aware that there is nevertheless an inner life, have fallen gradually into abstractions concerning everything of significance to the human soul.

To be clear regarding this difficult matter, let us recall something very significant that was learnt in the Mysteries. How many people to-day believe in their innermost consciousness: 'If I think something—for instance, if I entertain a bad thought about my neighbour—it has no significance for the outer world; the thought is only in myself. It has a quite different significance if I give him a box on the ears. This is something that happens on the physical plane; the other is a mere feeling or a mere thought.' Or again, how many people there are who, when they fall into a sin or a lie or an error, say: 'This is something that happens in the human soul.' And, by contrast, if a stone falls from the roof: 'This is something that takes place externally.' And they will readily explain, using crude sense-concepts, that when a stone falls, perhaps accidentally, into water, it sets up ripples which spread out far and wide, so that everything produces effects which continue unobserved; but anything that has occurred in the soul is shut off from the world outside. People could therefore come to believe that to sin, to err, and then to put it right again, is entirely a concern of the individual soul. To anyone with an outlook of this kind, something many of us have witnessed in the last two years must seem grotesque.

Let me recall to you the scene in the Rosicrucian drama, *The Portal of Initiation,* where Capesius and Strader enter the astral world, and it is shown that what they think, speak and feel is not without significance for the objective world, the Macrocosm, but actually releases storms in the elements. For modern man it is absurd to suppose that destructive forces can strike at the Macrocosm through somebody having had wrong thoughts. In the Mysteries it was made very clear to the pupil that when, for example anyone tells a lie or falls into error, this is a real process which does not concern himself only. The Germans say 'Thoughts are duty free', because they see no Customs barrier when the thoughts arise. Thoughts belong to the objective world; they are not merely experiences of the soul. The pupil of the Mystery saw: 'When you tell a lie, it signifies in the supersensible world the darkening of a certain light; when you perpetrate a loveless action, something in the spiritual world is burnt up in the fire of lovelessness; with errors you extinguish light in the Macrocosm.' The effect was shown to the pupil through objective experience: how, through an error, something is extinguished on the astral plane, and darkness follows; or how through a loveless action something acts like a burning and destroying fire.

In exoteric life man does not know what is going on around him. He is like an ostrich with its head in the sand; he does not see effects which nevertheless are there. The effects of feeling are there, and they would be visible to supersensible sight if the man were led into the Mysteries. It was not until the nineteenth century that anyone could say: 'Everything in which a man has sinned, everything in which he is weak, is his personal affair only. Redemption must come about through an experience in the soul, and so Christ also can be only an experience in the soul.' What is necessary, in order that man may not only find his way to Christ, but that he may not sunder his connection with the Macrocosm, is the knowledge: 'If you incur error and sin, these are objective, not subjective events, and because of them something happens outside in the Cosmos.' And in the moment when a

man becomes conscious that with his sin, with his error,
something objective happens; when he knows that what he
has done, what he has given out from himself, is not connected merely with himself but with the whole objective
course of cosmic development, then he will no longer be able
to say to himself that compensation for what he has brought
about is only an inner concern of the soul. There is indeed a
good and significant possibility that a man who sees that
thoughts and feelings are objective may also see that what
has brought and brings people into mistakes through successive earth-lives is not an inward affair related to a single life,
but is the consequence of karma.

Now an event which was outside history and outside
human responsibility, as was the Luciferic influence in the
old Lemurian period, could not possibly be expunged from
the world by a human event. Through the Luciferic event
man gained a great benefit: he became a free being. But he
also incurred a liability: the propensity to deviate from the
path of the good and the right, and from the path of the true.
What has happened in the course of incarnations is a matter
of karma. But all that has crept down from the Macrocosm
into the Microcosm, all that the Luciferic forces have given
to man, is something that man cannot deal with by himself.
To compensate for the objective Luciferic event, another
objective act was needed. In short, man must feel that what
he incurs as error and sin is not merely subjective, and that
an experience in the soul which is merely subjective is not
sufficient to bring about Redemption.

Anyone who is convinced of the objectivity of error will
thus understand also the objectivity of the act of Redemption. One cannot by any means treat the Luciferic influence
as an objective act without treating in the same manner the
compensating act, the Event of Golgotha. A theosophist can
only choose between two things. Everything may be set on
the foundation of karma; of course that is quite right as
regards everything that man himself has brought about.

But then we come to the necessity of stretching out the repeated lives forward and backward as far as we like, with no end to it in either direction. It always goes round and round like a wheel. The other thing—the alternative choice —is the concrete idea of evolution we must hold: that there was a Saturn, a Sun, and a Moon existence which were quite different from the Earth existence; that in the Earth existence the kind of repeated earth-life as we know it first occurred; that the Luciferic event was a single unrepeated event—all this alone gives real content to our theosophical outlook. All this, however, is inconceivable without the objectivity of the Event of Golgotha.

In pre-Christian times men were—as you know—different in various ways. One particular difference was that when they came down from spiritual worlds into earthly incarnations they brought with them, as substance, some of the Divine element. For this reason, when a man reflected on his own weakness, he always felt that the best part of him had originated in the Divine sphere from which he had descended. But the Divine element gradually became exhausted in the course of further incarnations, and it was quite exhausted when the Events of Palestine drew near. The last after-effects of it continued to be felt, but none of it was left when John the Baptist declared: 'Change your conception of the world, for the times have changed. Now you will no longer be able to rise up into the spiritual as in the past, for the vision that could see into the old spirituality is lost. Change your thinking, and accept the Divine Being who is to give anew to men what they have had to lose through their descent to earth!' Consequently—you may deny this if you think in the abstract, but not if you look at history in concrete terms— the feelings and perceptions of men changed altogether at the turning-point of the old and new epochs, a point marked by the Events of Palestine.

After these events, men began to feel forsaken. They felt forsaken when they approached the hardest questions, those

which concerned most directly the innermost part of the
soul; when, for example, they asked themselves: 'What will
become of me when I go through the gate of death with a
number of deeds that have not been made good?' Then there
came to meet them a thought which certainly might be born
from the longing of the soul, but could be allayed only when
the soul could say to itself: 'Yes, a Being has lived who
entered into the evolution of mankind and to whom you can
hold fast. He is working in the outer Cosmos, where you
cannot go. He is working to bring about compensation for
your deeds. He will help you to make good the evil results of
the Luciferic influence!' Through this feeling oneself forsaken, and then feeling oneself rescued by an objective
power, there enters into humanity an intuitive feeling that
sin is a real power, an objective fact, and that the Act of
Redemption is also objective, an act that cannot be accomplished by an individual, for he has not invoked the Luciferic
influence, but only by One who works in the worlds where
Lucifer is consciously active.

All that I have thus set before you, in words drawn from
Spiritual Science, was not grasped intellectually, as knowledge. It resided in feelings and intuitive perceptions, and
from this source came the need to turn to Christ. For those
who felt this need there was of course the possibility of finding
in Christian communities ways by which they could deepen
all such perceptions and feelings.

After man had lost his primal connection with the Gods,
what did he find when he looked out at the material world?
Through his descent into the material realm, his perception
of the spiritual, of the physical manifestation of the Divine
in the cosmos, steadily declined. The remnants of the old
clairvoyance faded by degrees, and nature, for him, was in
a certain sense deprived of the Divine. A merely material
world was spread out before him. And in face of this material
universe he could in no way maintain a belief that the
Christ-Principle was at work there. The nineteenth-century

Kant-Laplace theory, whereby our solar system developed out of a cosmic nebula, and eventually life arose on individual planets, has led finally to the universe being regarded as a collaboration of atoms. If we try to think of Christ in this setting, as conceived by materialistic scientists, it makes no sense. There is no place for the Christ-Being in this cosmogony, no place for anything spiritual. You remember someone saying—I read you the passage—that he would have to tear up his whole conception of the universe if he had to believe in the Resurrection. This shows that in contemplating Nature, or in thinking about Nature, all possibility of penetrating into the living essence of natural facts has disappeared.

When I speak like this, it is not by way of disapproval. The time had to come when Nature would be deprived of the Divine, deprived of the Spirit, so that man could formulate the totality of abstract thoughts required to comprehend external nature, as the outlook of Copernicus, Kepler and Galileo enabled him to do. The web of thoughts which has led to our age of machinery had to take hold of humanity. On the other hand, it was necessary that this age should have a compensation for the fact that it had become impossible in exoteric life to find a direct path from the Earth to the spiritual. For if man had been able to find this path, he would have been able to find the path to Christ, as he will find it in the coming centuries. There had to be a compensation.

The question now is: What had become necessary as an exoteric path for man to Christ during the centuries in which an atomistic conception of the universe became gradually accepted, a conception which alienated Nature more and more from the Divine and in the nineteenth century grew into the study of nature deprived of the Divine?

A two-fold remedy was required. A spiritual vision of the Christ could be found exoterically in two ways. One way was to show that all matter is completely foreign to man's inner spiritual being. He could be shown that it is untrue to say that everywhere in space where matter appears, *only* matter is present. How could this come about? In no other way than by something being given to man which is at one and the same time spirit and matter; something which he knows is spirit and yet sees to be matter. Therefore the transformation, the eternally valid transformation, of spirit into matter, of matter into spirit, had to continue as a vital fact. And this came to pass because the Holy Communion has been celebrated, has been maintained through the centuries as a Christian ritual. And the further we go back in the centuries towards the institution of the Holy Communion, the more can we trace how in the older times, not yet so materialistic, it was better understood.

In regard to higher things, when people begin to discuss something, it is a proof, as a rule, that they no longer understand it. Even simple matters, as long as they are understood, are not much discussed. Discussions are a proof that the point at issue is not understood by a majority of the people involved. Thus it was with the Holy Communion. As long as it was known that the Holy Communion furnished a living proof that matter is not merely matter, but that there are ceremonial acts through which the spirit can be united with matter—as long as people knew that this interpenetration of matter with spirit, as it finds expression in the Holy Communion, is a union with the Being of Christ, so long was the Holy Communion accepted without argument. But then came the time when Materialism arose, when people no longer understood what lies at the foundation of the Holy Communion. Then they disputed whether the bread and wine are merely symbols of the Divine, or whether Divine power actually flows into them. For anyone who can see more deeply, all the disputes which arose on this account at the beginning of the new epoch signify that the original understanding of the ritual had been lost. For those who desired to come to Christ, the Holy Communion was a complete equivalent of the esoteric path, if they could not take

that path, and thus in the Holy Communion they could find
a real union with Christ. For all things have their time.
Certainly, just as it is true in regard to the spiritual life that a
quite new age is dawning, so is it true that the way to Christ
which for centuries was the right one for many people will
remain for centuries more the right one for many. Things
pass over gradually into one another, and what was formerly
right will gradually pass over into something else when
people are ready for it.

The aim of Theosophy is to work in such a way that we
shall grasp in the spirit itself something concrete, something
real. By means of meditation, concentration and all that we
learn as the knowledge of higher worlds, men become ripe in
their inner being not merely to experience thought-worlds, or
worlds of abstract feelings and perceptions, but to permeate
themselves inwardly with the element of the Spirit; thereby
they will experience the Communion in the Spirit; thereby
thoughts, meditative thoughts, will be able to live in man;
they will even be the very same, only from within outwards,
as the symbol of the Holy Communion, the consecrated
Bread, has been from without inwards. And as the un-
developed Christian can seek his way to Christ through the
Holy Communion, so the developed Christian who, through
progressive knowledge of the Spirit has learnt to know the
Form of the Christ, can raise himself in spirit to what will
indeed be in the future an exoteric path for men. That will be
the force which is to bring to men a widening of the Christ-
Impulse. But then all ceremonies will change, and that
which formerly came to pass through the attributes of
bread and wine will come about in the future through a
spiritual Communion. The *thought* of the Sacrament, the
Holy Communion, will remain. Only it must be made possible that certain thoughts which flow to us through what is
imparted within our Movement, certain inner thoughts and
feelings, shall permeate and spiritualise our inner being—
thoughts and feelings as fully consecrated as in the best sense

of inner Christian development the Holy Communion has spiritualised the human soul and filled it with the Christ.

When this becomes possible—and it will be possible—we shall have progressed a stage further in evolution. And then we shall see the real proof that Christianity is greater than its external form. For a poor opinion of Christianity is held by anyone who thinks it will be obliterated when the external forms of the Christianity of a certain period are swept away. A true opinion will be permeated with the conviction that all Churches which have cherished the Christ-Thought, all external thoughts, all external forms, are temporal and therefore transitory, while the Christ-Thought will live in ever-new forms in the hearts and souls of men in the future, little as these new forms are evident to-day. Thus we are first taught by Spiritual Science how, along one exoteric path, the Holy Communion had its significance in earlier times.

The other exoteric path was through the Gospels. And here again we must realise what in earlier times the Gospels still were for men. It is not very long since the Gospels were not read as they were in the nineteenth century. In those days they were read as a life-giving fountain whence something substantial passed over into the soul. They were not read in the way described in the first lecture of this course, when we were speaking of a false path, but so that a person saw approaching from outside something for which his soul was panting with thirst; they were so read that his soul found pictured therein the real Redeemer, of whom the soul knew that He must be there, in the wide universe.

Those who understood how to read the Gospels in this way never thought of asking the endless questions which first became questions for the intelligent, clever people of the nineteenth century. You need only recall how many times in speaking of these questions, in one form or another, we have had to say that for quite clever people, who have all science and learning at their finger tips, the thought of Christ Jesus and the Events of Palestine are truly not compatible with the modern conception of the universe. In an apparently enlightened way they say that when men were not aware that the earth is a quite small heavenly body, they could believe that with the Cross of Golgotha a special new event took place on earth. But since Copernicus taught that the earth is a planet like others, can one still believe that Christ came to us from another planet? Why should we believe that the earth is so exceptionally situated as was formerly thought? A simile is then brought in: 'Since our conception of the universe has been so much enlarged, it seems as though one of the most important artistic presentations had taken place, not on the great stage of a capital city, but on the small stage of some provincial theatre.' So that is how it looks to these people: the earth is such an insignificant little cosmic body that the Events of Palestine appear like the performance of a great cosmic drama on the stage of a small provincial theatre. We can no longer imagine such a thing, because the earth is so small in comparison with the great universe!

It seems so clever when something like that is said, but after all there is not much cleverness in it, for Christianity never asserted what is here apparently contradicted. Christianity has never placed the beginning of the Christ-Impulse in the magnificent places of the earth. It has always seen a certain deep seriousness in the fact that the bearer of the Christ was born in a stable among poor shepherds. Not only the little earth, but a very obscure place on earth, was sought out in Christian tradition to place the Christ therein. Christianity from the very first answered the questions of the clever people. But they have not understood the answers which Christianity itself has given, because they could no longer let the living force of the great majestic pictures work upon the soul.

Nevertheless, through the Gospel pictures alone, without the Holy Communion and all that is connected with it—for the Holy Communion stands at the centre of all Christian cults—an exoteric path to Christ could not have been found. For the Gospels could not then have been widely enough popularised for a finding of the way to Christ to depend on them alone. And when the Gospels were popularised, we can see that it was not an unmixed blessing. For at the same time arose the great misunderstanding of the Gospels: they were taken superficially, and then all that the nineteenth century made of them came about; and indeed—speaking quite objectively—it was bad enough. I think anthroposophists will understand what is meant here by 'bad enough'. No censure is intended, for we cannot but acknowledge the diligence which the nineteenth century brought to the task of scientific investigation, including all the work in natural science. The tragedy is that this very science—and anyone familiar with it will grant this—owing to its deep seriousness and its tremendous, devoted industry, which one can only admire, has led to a complete splitting up and destruction of what it wished to teach. When in the future course of evolution people look back at our time, they will feel it to be particularly tragic that men sought to conquer the Bible by means of a science worthy of endless admiration —and succeeded only in losing the Bible.

Thus we can see that as regards these two aspects of the exoteric we are living in a transitional period, and in so far as we have grasped the spirit of Theosophy, the old paths must lead over into others. And having now considered the exoteric paths of the past to the Christ-Impulse, we shall see to-morrow how this relationship to Christ takes form in the realm of the esoteric. We will then conclude our study by showing how we can come to grasp the Christ-Event not only for the whole evolution of humanity, but for each individual man. We shall be able to review the esoteric path more briefly, because we have assembled building-stones for it during past years. We will crown our endeavours by fixing our gaze upon the relationship of the Christ-Impulse to every individual human soul.

LECTURE X

Yesterday we tried to characterise the path to Christ that can still be taken to-day, as it could especially in earlier times, by exoteric means. We will now touch briefly on the esoteric path—the path which leads to Christ in such a way that he can be found within the supersensible worlds.

First of all we must note that this esoteric path to Christ Jesus was also the way of the Evangelists, of those who wrote the Gospels. For although the writer of the John Gospel had himself witnessed many of the events he describes—as you can see from the lecture-cycle on this Gospel—his chief object was not merely to relate what he remembered, for this applies only to those minute, exact details which surprise us in his Gospel. The great, majestic, crowning features of the work of redemption, of the Mystery of Golgotha, were drawn by the writer of this Gospel from his clairvoyant consciousness also. Consequently, although the Gospels are really revived Mystery rituals—this is shown in my *Christianity as Mystical Fact*—they are so because the writers of the Gospels, following their esoteric path, could procure for themselves out of the supersensible world a picture of the events in Palestine which led to the Mystery of Golgotha. Ever since the Mystery of Golgotha up to our own times, a person who desired to come to a supersensible experience of the Christ-Event had to go through the stages which you will find described in earlier lecture-cycles as the seven stages of our Christian Initiation: The Washing of the Feet; The Scourging; The Crowning with Thorns; The Mystic Death; The Burial; the Resurrection; the Ascension. To-day we will make clear to ourselves what the pupil can attain by going through this Christian Initiation.

First of all, one essential point. As you can convince yourselves by reading the lectures on this subject, Christian Initiation is very different from the incorrect method of Initiation described in the first lecture of this course. In Christian Initiation certain feelings which belong to humanity in general are first invoked, and they lead to an Imagination of the Washing of the Feet. Thus the picture of this in the John Gospel is not the first thing to be imagined; the aspirant begins by trying to live for a long time with certain feelings and perceptions. I have often characterised this by saying that the person concerned should gaze upon the plant, which grows out of the mineral ground, takes into itself the materials of the mineral kingdom, and yet raises itself above this kingdom as a higher being than the mineral. If the plant could speak and feel, it would bow down to the mineral kingdom and say: 'Certainly I was destined within the economy of the Cosmos to attain a higher stage than you, Mineral, but you give me the possibility of existence. In the order of beings you are certainly a lower being than myself, but I have to thank you for my existence, and I bow myself in humility before you.' In the same way the animal would have to bow down to the plant, although the plant is a lower being than the animal, and say: 'I thank you for my existence; I acknowledge it in humility, and I bow myself before you.' And so would each being that climbs upwards have to bow down to the other standing below, and also he who has risen by way of a spiritual ladder to a higher level must bow down to the beings who alone have made this possible for him.

A person who permeates himself with the feeling of humility in regard to the lower, who thoroughly incoporates this feeling in his own being and lets it live there for months, perhaps even for years, will see that it spreads itself out in his organism, and so pervades him that he experiences a transformation of this feeling into an Imagination. And this Imagination corresponds exactly to the scene represented in the John Gospel as the Washing of the Feet, where Christ Jesus, who is the Head of the Twelve, stoops to those who stand here below Him in the order of the physical world, and in humility acknowledges that He thanks those who are below Him for the possibility of his higher ascent. He acknowledges before the Twelve: 'As the animal thanks the plant, so do I thank you for what I was able to become in the physical world!' A person who permeates himself with this feeling comes not only to an Imagination of the Washing of the Feet, but also to a quite pronounced feeling, as though water were washing over his feet. This can be felt for weeks: it shows how deeply imbued our human nature is with such universal human feelings, which nevertheless can raise man above himself.

Further, we have seen that we can go through the experience which leads to the Imagination of the Scourging when we place the following vividly before us: 'Much suffering and pain will meet me in the world; yes, from all sides suffering and pain may come; no one escapes them. But I will so steel my will that suffering and pain, the scourgings that come from the world, may do their worst; I will stand upright and bear my fate resignedly, as it comes to pass. For had it not come to pass as it has done, as I have experienced it, I should not have been able to reach the height I have attained.' When the person in question makes this a matter of his perception, and lives within it, he actually feels something like sharp pains and woundings, like strokes of a scourge against his own skin, and the Imagination arises as if he were outside himself, and was watching himself scourged according to the example of Christ Jesus. In line with this example one can experience the Crowning of Thorns, the Mystic Death, and so on. This has often been described.

What is attained by a man who thus seeks within himself to experience first the four stages, and then, when his karma is favourable, the others also, making in all seven stages of Christian Initiation? From the foregoing description you can gather that the whole scale of feelings we go through ought to strengthen us and give us power, and ought to make us into quite another nature, so that in the world we feel ourselves standing strong, powerful and free, and also capable of every act of devoted love. In Christian Initiation, this ought in a deep sense to become a second nature to us. For what has to happen?

Perhaps it has not yet occurred to all those of you who have read the earlier elementary cycles, and so have met with Christian Initiation in its seven stages, that owing to the intensity of the experiences which must be undergone, the effects go right into the physical body. For through the strength and power with which we go through these feelings, it really is at first as if water were washing over our feet, and then as if we were transfixed with wounds. We actually feel as if thorns were pressing into our head; we feel all the pain and suffering of the Crucifixion. We have to feel this before we can experience the Mystical Death, the Burial and the Resurrection, as these also have been described. Even if we have not gone through these feelings with sufficient intensity, they will certainly have the effect that we become strong and full of love in the right sense of the word. But what we then incorporate can go only as far as the etheric body.

When, however, we begin to feel that our feet are as though washed with water, our body as if covered with wounds, then we have succeeded in driving these feelings so deeply into our nature that they have penetrated as far as the physical body. They do indeed penetrate the physical body, and then the stigmata, the marks of the bleeding wounds of Christ Jesus, may appear. We drive the feelings inwards into the physical body and know that they develop their strength in the physical body itself. We consciously feel ourselves more in the grip of our whole being than if the impressions were merely in the astral body and etheric body. The essential thing is that through a process of mystical feeling we work right into our physical body; and when we do this we are doing nothing less than making ourselves ready in our physical body to receive the Phantom that went forth from the grave on Golgotha. Hence we work into our physical body in order to make it so living that it feels a relationship with, an attractive force towards, the Phantom that rose out of the grave on Golgotha.

And here I would make an incidental remark. In Spiritual Science one must accustom oneself to becoming acquainted with cosmic secrets and cosmic truths *gradually*. Anyone who is not prepared to wait for the relevant truths will not make good progress. Of course people would like to have Spiritual Science all at once, preferably in one book or in one course of lectures. But that cannot be so, as you will see from an example. How long is it since in earlier lectures Christian Initiation was first described? You heard that such and such takes place, and that the individual, through the feelings which affect his soul, works right into his physical body. Everything said in those earlier lectures was intended to provide some elements for understanding the Mystery of Golgotha, and now for the first time it is possible to describe how an individual, through the requisite exercises of feeling in the course of Christian Initiation, makes himself ripe to receive the Phantom which rose from the grave of Golgotha. We had to wait until the union of the subjective with the objective could be found; and for this many preparatory lectures were necessary. Even to-day there are many things that can be indicated only as 'half truths'. Anyone who has patience to continue with us—whether in this or in another incarnation, each according to his karma—will have seen how he could advance from the description of the mystical path in the Christian sense to the description of the objective fact, and so to the real meaning of this Christian Initiation, and he will see also that still higher truths will be brought to light from out of Spiritual Science in the course of the coming years or the next age. Thus we see the aim, the goal, of Christian Initiation.

Through what has been characterised as Rosicrucian Initiation, i.e. what an individual can have of it as Initiation to-day, the same thing in a certain sense is also attained, only by somewhat different means. A bond of attraction is formed between the individual, in so far as he is incorporated in a physical body, and that which arose as the real proto-type of the physical body from the grave of Golgotha. Now we know from previous lectures that we are at the starting-point of a world-epoch in which we must expect an event that will not take place on the physical plane, as did the Event of Golgotha, but in the supersensible world; an event which nevertheless stands in a close and true connection with the Event of Golgotha. The latter was designed to give back to man his real physical force-body, the Phantom which had degenerated from the beginning of the Earth-evolution, and for the giving back of it a series of events on the physical plane had to occur; but for that which is now to happen an event on the physical plane is not necessary. An incarnation of the Christ-Being in a human body of flesh could take place only *once* in the course of the Earth-evolution. When people announce a repetition of the incarnation of this Being, it simply means that the Christ-Being is not understood.

The event now to come, which can be observed only in a supersensible world, has been characterised in the words: 'Christ becomes for men the Lord of Karma.' This means that in future the ordering of karmic transactions will come about through Christ. Ever more and more will men of the future feel: 'I am going through the gate of death with my karmic account. On one side stand my good, clever and beautiful deeds, my clever, beautiful, good and intelli-gent thoughts; on the other side stands everything evil, wicked, stupid, foolish and loathsome. But He who in the future will have the office of Judge for the incarnations which will follow in human evolution, in order to bring order into this karmic account of men, is the Christ!' And truly we have to picture this in the following way:

After we have gone through the gate of death, we shall be incarnated again in a later period. We shall then have to encounter events through which our karma can be balanced, for every man must reap what he has sown. Karma is a just law. But what the karmic law has to fulfil is not there only for individual men. Karma does not only balance the accounts of each Ego, but in every case the balancing must be arranged so as to be in the best possible accord with the concerns of the whole world. It must enable us to give all possible help to the advancement of mankind on earth. For this we need enlightenment, not merely the knowledge that the karmic fulfilment of our deed must come about. The fulfilment can take a form which will be either less or more useful for the general progress of humanity. Hence we must choose those thoughts, feelings or perceptions which will pay off our karma and at the same time serve the collective progress of mankind. In the future it will fall to Christ to bring the balance of our karma into line with the general Earth-karma and the general progress of humanity. And this happens principally in the time between death and a new birth. But it will also be prepared for in the epoch of time we are now approaching, before whose door we stand, because men will more and more acquire the capacity for a special experience. Very few are capable of it now, but from the middle of this century onwards, through the next 1,000 years, more and more people will have the following experience.

A person has done this or that. He will feel constrained to reflect on his action, and something like a dream-picture, arising in his mind, will make a quite remarkable impression on him. He will say to himself: 'I cannot identify this as a recollection of something I have done, yet it feels like an experience of my own.' Like a dream-picture it will stand there before him, closely concerned with him; but he cannot recall that he has experienced or done it in the past. If he is an anthroposophist he will understand the matter;

otherwise he will have to wait until he comes to Anthroposophy and learns to understand it. The anthroposophist will
know: 'What you see as an apparent consequence of your
actions is a picture that will be fulfilled in the future; the
balancing of your actions is shown to you in advance.' We
are at the beginning of an epoch in which men, directly after
they have committed a deed, will have a premonition, a
feeling, perhaps even a significant picture, of how this deed
will be karmically balanced.

Thus, in closest connection with human experience,
enhanced capabilities for humanity will arise during the
coming epoch. These capabilities will give a powerful
stimulus to human morality, and this will signify something
quite different from the voice of conscience, which has been
a preparation for it. The individual will no longer believe:
'What I have done will die with me.' He will know quite
exactly: 'My action will not die when I die; it will have a
consequence which will live on with me.' And there is much
else that the individual will know. The time during which
the doors of the spiritual world have been closed to men is
nearly over. Men must again climb up into the spiritual
world. Their awakening capacities will enable them to
participate in the spiritual world. Clairvoyance will always
be different from this participation. Just as there was an
ancient dreamlike clairvoyance, so will there be a future
clairvoyance that is not dreamlike, the clairvoyance of people
who know what they are doing and what it signifies.

Something else, too, will come about. The individual will
know: 'I am not alone. Everywhere there are spiritual
beings who stands in a relationship to me.' Men will learn
to communicate with these beings and to live with them.
And in the next three thousand years the truth that Christ
is acting as Karmic Judge will become apparent to a
sufficiently large number of people. Christ Himself will be
experienced by men as an etheric Form. Like Paul before
Damascus, they will know quite intimately that Christ lives,

and is the Source for the reawakening of the physical prototype we received at the beginning of our evolution, and need if the Ego is to attain full development.

If through the Mystery of Golgotha something happened which gave the greatest impetus to human evolution, on the other hand it came at the time when the human mind, the human soul, were in their darkest condition. There were indeed ancient periods of evolution when men could know with certainty, because they had an ancestral memory, that the human individuality goes through repeated earth-lives. In the Gospels the teaching of repeated earth-lives is apparent only when we understand the Gospels and can discern traces of it there. That was the time when men were least fitted to comprehend this teaching. In the later times when men sought for Christ along the path indicated yesterday, everything had to take the form of a childlike preparation. Men could not then be made acquainted with experiences concerning reincarnation; they were not ripe for it and it would only have led them into error. Christianity had to develop for nearly 2,000 years without being able to indicate the teaching of reincarnation.

We have shown in these lectures how different it was in Buddhism, and how in Western consciousness the thought of repeated earth-lives arises as something self-evident. Certainly, many misunderstandings still prevail; but whether we take this idea from Lessing or from the psychologist Drossbach, we become aware that for the European consciousness the teaching of reincarnation concerns humanity at large, whereas in Buddhism the individual regards the question of how he goes from life to life, how he can free himself from the thirst for existence, as concerning only his personal inner life. The Oriental makes what is given to him as teaching about reincarnation into a path of individual redemption, whereas for Lessing the essential question was: 'How can the whole of humanity move forward?' According to Lessing, we must distinguish successive periods of time within the progressive development of humanity. Something new is given to humanity in each epoch. We see from history that new civilising actions keep on emerging in the course of human development. How could one speak of the evolution of the whole of humanity, says Lessing, if a soul lived in only one epoch? Whence could the fruits of civilisation come if human beings were not born again, if what they had learnt in one epoch were not carried over into the next, and its fruits into the following epoch and so on?

Thus for Lessing the idea of repeated earth-lives is not only a concern of the individual soul. It concerns the whole course of earthly civilisation. And in order that an advanced civilisation may arise, a soul which lives in the nineteenth century must carry over into its present existence whatever it had previously gained. For the sake of the earth and its civilisation, human beings must be born again. That is Lessing's thought. But in this thought of reincarnation as concerning all mankind the Christ-Impulse has been at work, woven into it. For the Christ-Impulse makes everything a man does or can do into an action of universal relevance, not something that touches him only as an individual. He only can be Christ's disciple who says: 'I do it for the least of the brethren, because I know Thou feelest as though I had done it for Thee.' As the whole of humanity is bound up with Christ, so does he who confesses Christ feel that he belongs to all mankind. This thought has worked into the thinking, feeling and perception of the whole human race. And when the idea of reincarnation reappeared in the eighteenth century, it appeared as a Christian thought. And although Widenmann treated reincarnation clumsily, in an embryonic way, yet in his prize essay of 1851 his thought of reincarnation is permeated by the Christian impulse. He devotes a special chapter to showing the connection between Christianity and the teaching of reincarnation.

It was necessary in human evolution that souls should first

accept the other Christian impulses, so that the thought of reincarnation might come to our consciousness in a ripe form. And indeed this thought of reincarnation will so connect itself with Christianity that it will be felt as something that leads a person on through successive incarnations. We shall understand how individuality, which is completely lost according to the Buddhist view—as we saw from the conversation of King Milinda with the sage Nagasena—first receives its true content by becoming permeated with Christ. We can now understand why the Buddhist view, about 500 years before the appearance of Christ, lost the human Ego, while retaining the teaching of successive incarnations. We have reached a time in which the human organism must understand, accept, permeate itself with the thought of reincarnation. For the progress of human evolution does not depend on what teachings are promulgated or find a new foothold. Other laws come into consideration, and they do not depend upon ourselves.

In the future human nature will develop certain powers which will have the effect that the individual, as soon as he has reached a certain age and has become properly conscious of himself, will have the feeling: 'There is something in me which I must understand.' This feeling will take hold of men more and more. In past times, even when human beings were fully aware of themselves, the consciousness which is now to come did not exist. It will express itself somewhat as follows: 'I feel something within me which is connected with my personal ego. Strangely, it will not fit in with all that I have come to know since birth.' One man will understand what is at work here; another will not. A man will understand it if he has carried the teachings of Spiritual Science into his life. Then he will know: 'What I am now feeling is foreign to me, because it is the ego that has come over from earlier lives.' This will oppress the heart, will cause fear and anxiety, in those who cannot explain it by repeated earth-lives. These feelings, which are not merely a theoretical uncertainty but a starving, a cramping, of life, will disappear through the perceptions given to us by Spiritual Science, which tell us: 'You must think of your life as extended over earlier earth-lives.' Then men will see what it means for them to experience the connection with the Christ-Impulse. For it is the Christ-Impulse which will give life to the whole retrospective view, the whole perspective of the past. A man will feel: 'Here was this incarnation; there, that one.' Then he will come to a time beyond which he will be unable to go without clearly understanding: 'The Christ-Impulse was then on earth!' Incarnations will be followed further back to a time when the Christ-Event was not yet there. This illumination of the retrospective view through the Christ-Impulse will be needed by men for their assurance in the future, as a necessity and a help which can flow into later incarnations.

This transformation of the human soul will derive from the Event which begins in the twentieth century and may be called the second Christ-Event, so that those persons in whom higher faculties have awakened will look upon the Lord of Karma. Some of you may say that when the Christ-Event of the twentieth century takes place, many of those now living will be with those who have fallen asleep, will be in the time between death and a new birth. But whether a person is living in a physical body, or in the time between death and a new birth, if he has prepared himself for the Christ-Event, he will experience it. The vision of the Christ-Event does not depend on whether we are incarnated in a physical body, but the preparation for the Christ-Event does so depend. Just as it was necessary that the first Christ-Event should take place on the physical plane in order that the salvation of man could be accomplished, so must the preparation be made here in the physical world, the preparation to look with full understanding, with full illumination, upon the Christ-Event of the twentieth century. For a person who looks upon it unprepared, when his powers have been awakened, will not be able to understand it. The Lord of Karma will then appear to him as a fearful judgment. In order to have an illuminated understanding of this Event, the individual must be prepared. The spreading abroad of the anthroposophical world-conception has taken place in our time for this purpose, so that men can be prepared on the physical plane to perceive the Christ-Event either on the physical plane or on the higher planes. Those who are not sufficiently prepared on the physical plane, and then go unprepared through the life between death and a new birth, will have to wait until, in the next incarnation, they can be further prepared through Anthroposophy for the understanding of Christ. During the next 3,000 years the opportunity will be given to men of going through this preparation, and the purpose of all anthroposophical development will be to render men more and more capable of participating in that which is to come.

Thus we understand how the past flows over into the future. When, for example, we recall how the Buddha permeated the astral body of the Nathan Jesus-child, we see how the activity of the Buddha forces continued after he himself no longer needed to incarnate again on earth. And when we remember how influences not directly connected with the Buddha worked on in the West, we see how the spiritual world penetrates the physical.

All this preparation is connected with the fact that men are always drawing nearer to an ideal which dawned in ancient Greece, an ideal formulated by Socrates: that when a man grasps the idea of the good, the moral, the ethical, he feels this idea as so magical an impulse that he becomes capable of living in accordance with it as an ideal. To-day we are not so far advanced that this ideal can be realised; we are only so far on that in certain circumstances a man may very well form a concept of the good; he may be very clever and wise, and yet he need not be morally good. The direction of inner evolution, however, is such that the ideas we hold of the good will immediately become moral impulses. That is the intent of the evolution we shall experience in the approaching times. And the teachings given on earth will increasingly be such that in the course of future centuries and millennia human speech will come to have an effect unimaginably greater than it has now or ever had in the past. To-day in the higher worlds anyone can see clearly the connection between intellect and morality; but as yet there is no human speech which works so magically that when a moral principle is stated, it sinks down into a man as a new idea, so that he perceives it as directly moral, and cannot do otherwise than act upon it as a moral impulse. After the next 3,000 years it will be possible to use a form of speech that could not now be entrusted to our heads. It will be such that everything intellectual will at the same time be moral, and this moral element will penetrate into the hearts of men. During the next 3,000 years the human race must become as though permeated with magical morality. Otherwise men would not be able to bear such an evolution; they would only misuse it.

For the special preparation of an evolution of this kind we must look at a much slandered individuality who lived about a century before our era. He is mentioned, though certainly in a distorted form, in Hebrew writings as Jeschu Ben Pandira—Jesus the son of Pandira. From lectures once given in Berne, some of you will know that this Jeschu Ben Pandira worked in preparation for the Christ-Event by training pupils, among whom was one who became the teacher of the writer of the Gospel of Matthew. Jeschu Ben Pandira, a noble Essene figure, preceded Jesus of Nazareth by a century. Jesus of Nazareth Himself only went among the Essenes, whereas Jeschu Ben Pandira was altogether an Essene.

Who was Jeschu Ben Pandira?

The successor of that Bodhisattva who in his final earthly incarnation had risen in his twenty-ninth year to be Gautama

Buddha was incorporated in the physical body of Jeschu Ben Pandira. Every Bodhisattva who rises to the rank of a Buddha has a successor. This oriental tradition corresponds exactly with occult research. The Bodhisattva who worked at that time in preparation for the Christ-Event was re-embodied again and again. One of his re-embodiments is fixed for the twentieth century. It is impossible to speak here more exactly concerning the re-embodiment of this Bodhisattva; something, however, can be said about the way in which such a Bodhisattva may be recognised.

Through a law which will be demonstrated and explained in future lectures, it is a peculiarity of this Bodhisattva that when he reappears in a new embodiment—and he always reappears thus in the course of the centuries—he is quite dissimilar in his youth from what he comes to be in his later activities. At a quite definite point of time in the life of this Bodhisattva, something like a revolution, a great trans-formation, always takes place. To express it more in detail, in some place or other there is a more or less gifted child, in whom it is not noticeable that he has to do anything special in preparation for the future evolution of humanity. Occult research confirms that no one during his childhood and youth gives so little sign of what he really is as he who is to incorporate a Bodhisattva. For at a certain point of time in his life a great change comes over him. If an individuality from the remote past—Moses, for example—is incorporated, it is not the same with him as it was with the Christ individ-uality, to whom Jesus of Nazareth left the sheaths. In the case of a Bodhisattva there certainly will be something like an exchange, but the individuality remains in a certain sense, and the individuality who comes from the remote past—as patriarch or another—and is to bring new forces for the evolution of humanity, descends, and the human being who receives him experiences an immense transformation. This transformation occurs particularly between the thirtieth and thirty-third years. It can never be known beforehand that this body will be taken possession of by the Bodhisattva. The change never shows itself in youth. The distinctive feature is precisely that the later years are so unlike the youthful ones.

He who was incorporated in Jeschu Ben Pandira—the Bodhisattva who was repeatedly reincarnated, and who succeeded Gautama Buddha—has prepared himself for his Bodhisattva-incarnation so that he can reappear and rise to the Buddha dignity exactly 5,000 years after the illumination of Gautama Buddha under the bodhi-tree. Here again occult investigation fully agrees with oriental tradition. So, 3,000 years from now, this Bodhisattva, looking back on all that has happened in the new epoch, and looking back on the Christ-Impulse and all that is connected with it, will speak in such a way that his speech will make into a reality what has just been characterised: intellectuality will become directly moral. The future Bodhisattva, who will place all that he has at the service of the Christ-Impulse, will be a Bringer of the Good through the Word, through the Logos. He will speak in a language as yet possessed by no man, but a language which is so holy that he who speaks it can be called a Bringer of the Good. This also will not show itself in his youth, but approximately in his thirty-first year he will appear as a new man, and will yield himself up as the one who can be filled with a higher individuality. The experience of one *single* incarnation in the flesh holds good only for Christ Jesus. All Bodhisattvas go through various successive incarnations on the physical plane. This Bodhisattva, 3,000 years hence, will have advanced so far that he will be a Bringer of the Good, a Maitreya Buddha, who will place his Words of Goodness at the service of the Christ-Impulse, which a sufficient number of men will by then have made part of their lives. The perspective of the future development of man tells us this to-day.

What was necessary so that human beings could come

gradually to this epoch of evolution? This we can make clear as follows.

If we wish to make a graphic picture of what happened in ancient Lemuria for the earth-evolution of man, we can say: That was the time when man descended from Divine Heights: it was ordained for him that he should develop further in a certain way, but through the Luciferic influence he was cast down more deeply into matter than he would have been without that influence. Thereby his path in evolution became different.

When man had gone downwards to the lowest stage, a powerful impetus in the upward direction was required. This impetus could come about only because in the higher worlds the Being whom we designate as the Christ-Being had formed a resolution which He would not have needed to take for His own evolution. For the Christ-Being would also have attained His evolution if He had taken a path far, far above the path that men were pursuing. He could have passed by, so to speak, far above the evolution of humanity. But if the upward impulse had not been given, human evolution would have been compelled to continue on its downward path. The Christ would have had an ascent, but humanity a downfall. Only because the Christ-Being had taken the resolution to unite Himself at the time of the Events of Palestine with a man, to embody Himself in a man and to make the upward path possible for humanity—only this could bring about the Redemption of humanity, as we may now call it: redemption from the impulse brought by the Luciferic forces and designated symbolically in the Bible as 'original sin', the Temptation by the Serpent and the original sin that was its consequence. Christ accomplished something that was not necessary for Himself.

What kind of Act was this?

It was an act of Divine Love. We must be quite clear that no human feeling is capable of realising the intensity of love that was needed for a God to make a decision—a decision

He had no need to make—to work upon earth in a human
body. Thereby, through an act of love, the most important
event in human evolution was brought about. And when
men grasp this act of love by a God, when they try to grasp it
as a great ideal in contrast with which every human act of
love can be but small, then, through this feeling of utter
disproportion between human love and the Divine Love
needed for the Mystery of Golgotha, they will draw near to
the building up, to the giving birth within them, of those
Imaginations which place before our spiritual gaze the
momentous Event of Golgotha. Yes, verily, it is possible to
attain to the Imagination of the mount on which the Cross
was raised, that Cross on which hung a God in human body,
a God who out of his own free will, out of Love, accomplished
the act whereby the earth and humanity could reach their
goal.

   If the God who is designated by the name of the Father
had not at one time permitted the Luciferic influences to
come to man, man would not have developed the free Ego.
With the Luciferic influence, the conditions for the free Ego
were established. That had to be permitted by the Father-
God. But just as the Ego, for the sake of freedom, had to become
entangled in matter, so then, in order that the Ego might be
freed from this entanglement, the entire love of the Son had
to lead to the Act of Golgotha. Through this alone the freedom of man, the complete dignity of man, first became
possible. For the fact that we can be free beings, we have to
thank a Divine Act of Love. As men we may feel free beings,
but we may never forget that for this freedom we have to
thank this Act of Love. Then, in the midst of our feeling, the
thought will arise: 'You can attain·to the value, the dignity,
of a man; but one thing you may not forget, that for being
what you are you have to thank Him who has brought back
to you your human prototype through the Redemption on
Golgotha.' Men should not be able to lay hold of the thought
of freedom without the thought of Redemption through

Christ: only then is the thought of freedom justified. If we will to be free, we must bring the offering of thanks to Christ for our freedom. Then only can we really perceive it. And those who consider that their dignity as men is restricted when they thank Christ for it, should recognise that human opinions have no significance in face of cosmic facts, and that one day they will very willingly acknowledge that their freedom was won by Christ.

*   *   *

What we have been able to do in these lectures is not very much for gaining a closer understanding of the Christ-Impulse, and of the whole course of human evolution on earth, from the standpoint of Spiritual Science. We can only bring together single building-stones. But if the effect upon our souls is something like a renewed stimulus to further effort, to further development along the path of knowledge, then these stones will have done their work for the great spiritual temple of humanity. And the best we can carry away from a spiritual-scientific study such as this is that once more we have learnt something towards a certain goal, that we have again somewhat enriched our knowledge. And our high goal is this: that we may know more exactly how much we still need to know. Then we shall be more and more permeated with the truth of the old Socratic saying: 'The more a man learns, the more he knows how little he knows.' But this conviction is good only when it is not a confession of passive, easy-going resignation, but testifies to a living will and effort towards an ever-extending knowledge. We ought not to acknowledge how little we know by saying, 'Since we cannot know everything, we would rather learn nothing; so let us fold our hands in our lap.' That would be a false result of spiritual-scientific study. The right result is to be more and more inspired to further striving; to regard every new thing learnt as a step towards the attainment of yet higher stages.

In these lectures we have perhaps had to say much about

the Redemption-thought without often using the word. This Redemption-thought should be felt by a seeker after the spirit as it was felt by a great forerunner of our Spiritual Science: that it is related and entrusted to our souls only as a consequence of our striving after the highest goals of knowing, feeling and willing. And as this great forerunner connects the word 'Redemption' with the word 'striving' and has expressed it in the line, 'Wer immer strebend sich bemüht, den können wir erlösen'—'He who never gives up striving, he it is whom we can redeem'—so should the anthroposophist always feel. The true Redemption can be grasped and felt and willed in its own realm only by some-one who never gives up.

May this lecture-cycle—which has been specially laid upon my heart, because so much has to be said in it con-cerning the Redemption-thought—be a stimulus to our further endeavours; may we find ourselves ever more and more united in our endeavours, during this incarnation and in later ones. May this be the fruit which comes from such studies. With this we will close, taking with us as a stimulus the thought that we must continually exert ourselves, in order that we may see what the Christ is, on the one hand, and on the other may draw nearer to Redemption, which is being set free not merely from the lower earth-path and earth-fate, but free also from everything that hinders man from attaining his dignity as man. But these things are written down truly only in the annals of the Spiritual. For the script that can be read in spiritual realms is the only true writing. Let us therefore strive to read the chapter concern-ing the dignity of man and the mission of man, in the script where these things stand written in the spiritual worlds.

APPENDIX

Public Lecture delivered at Karlsruhe
4th October, 1911

APPENDIX

Public Lecture delivered at Karlsruhe
4th October, 1911

As our subject is arousing the very widest interest everywhere, it seems justifiable to approach it from an anthroposophical standpoint. The manner in which it is being discussed and brought to public notice is, of course, very far removed from this point of view. If it is true that Anthroposophy is little understood and liked today, it may be said at once that the treating of this theme in an anthroposophical manner presents peculiar difficulties. It is unusual in our age for the feelings to be so attuned as to appreciate anthroposophical truths bearing on the more obvious matters of spiritual life, and it is directly repugnant to our present-day consciousness when a topic has to be discussed which calls for the application of Anthroposophy or spiritual science to the most difficult and holiest subjects.

It may be safely affirmed at the outset that the being around whom our thoughts are about to centre has been for many centuries the turning point of all thought and feeling, and moreover that He has called forth widely differing judgments, emotions and opinions. Countless are those who for centuries have held firmly as a rock to all that is connected with the name of Christ and of Jesus, beyond number also are pictures of Him which have moved souls and occupied thoughtful men ever since the Event in Palestine. Always the picture has been modified according to the general views of the times, to what was felt and considered true at any given period. Thus, when the way had been prepared by the intellectual currents of thought of the eighteenth century, it came about in the course of the following century that what could be intellectually grasped as 'Christ' withdrew into the background as compared with what was later called the 'Historical Jesus'. It is around the 'Historical Jesus' that the widespread controversy has arisen, and which has here in Karlsruhe its most important protagonists and its most vigorous combatants. For this reason it is as well to give a short indication of the current position of the controversy before entering on the subject of 'Christ Jesus'.

We might say that the Historical Jesus of nineteenth century thought originated under the influence of the intellectual current that takes a merely external view of spiritual life and judges it by means of external documents: that there is evidence of His having lived at the beginning of our era in Palestine, that He was crucified and, according to the faithful, rose again. It is quite in line with the character and nature of the present era, now approaching its termination, that in the case of theological research, faith limited itself to what it was thought could be confirmed by historical documents in the same way as any ordinary event is confirmed by independent writings. It may be said that all the historical written traditions elsewhere than in the New Testament could, in the opinion of one of the most important judges, be 'easily contained in a quarto page'. All the other references to the historical Jesus in any documents whatever, such as, for example, in Josephus or Tacitus, may be put out of court, for they can never be used from the standpoint of that historical science which holds good today. Beyond these there are only the Gospels and the Pauline Epistles. How did the historical research of the nineteenth century examine the Gospels? Regarded purely externally, how do they appear? If taken like other records, such as those of military engagements and so forth, they seem to be very contradictory documents of the physical plane, the fourfold presentation of which cannot be brought into harmony. In face of what we call historical criticism these records fall to pieces. For it must be allowed that everything which the earnest and diligent research of the nineteenth century collected out of the Gospels themselves, in order to gain a true picture of Jesus of Nazareth, has crumbled away through the presentation of the kind of research brought forward by Professor Drews. As to all that can be said against the Gospels as facts of history, it is evident that nothing can come to light about the person of Jesus of Nazareth if we apply the methods whereby accurate science and strict criticism ratify other historical facts. We can only be considered very dilettante scientists if we do not make this concession to the science of the day.

Is it not a possibility that those who in the nineteenth century presented the teaching of Jesus of Nazareth, and wanted to arrive at an historical portrait of Him, had an entirely false conception of the Gospels? Were the Gospels really intended to be historical records in the sense understood in the nineteenth century?

Whatever was to be said on this subject I endeavoured to state many years ago in my work, *Christianity as Mystical Fact*, and our present question, as to what was the real object of the Gospels, was intended to receive its answer not merely through the contents of that book but through the title itself. For the title was not 'The Mysticism of Christianity', nor 'The Mystical Contents of Christianity': its object was rather to show that Christianity in its origin and its whole being is not an external fact but a fact of the spiritual world, and one that can only be comprehended by an insight into a realm lying behind the world of sense and behind what can be corroborated by historical records. It was shown that the forces and causes which brought about the Event of Palestine were not to be found in that region wherein external historical events take place, and thus that possibly not only may Christianity have a mystical content but that Mysticism — the actual gazing into the spiritual — is necessary to disentangle the threads that were woven behind the Event in Palestine and made it possible.

In order to realize what Christianity is, and what it can and must be in the soul of man today if he is to understand it aright, let us see how deeply grounded in the spiritual facts of human development were the words of St. Augustine: 'That which we now call the Christian Religion already existed among the ancients and was never absent from the beginning of the human race up to the time when Christ appeared in the flesh, from which time forward the true religion which was already there received the name of the Christian Religion.' Thus does a standard authority point to the fact that it was not something new which came into humanity with the events of Palestine, but that in a certain sense a transformation had taken place in that which from time immemorial the souls of men had sought and striven for as knowledge. Something was given to humanity which had always been in existence, though hitherto along other lines than the Christian. If we wish to test the other way in which the preceding ages could come to the truths and wisdom of Christianity, we are referred by the historical development of humanity to the Mysteries of Antiquity or the Ancient Mysteries. What is meant by these expressions is little understood today, but it will become clearer the more men grasp the conception of the cosmos as presented by spiritual science.

Attention must be focussed not merely upon the external religions of the people of antiquity, but upon what was practised in pre-Christian times in those mystic abodes designated by the name of the Mysteries. In the book *Occult Science* an explanation is to be found from the aspect of spiritual science, and there are also numbers of secular writers who have declared publicly what was the secret of mankind in antiquity. We read that only a few were admitted to the schools which were designated 'The Mysteries', and that these schools were the homes of the cults. Also there was a small circle of men admitted to the Mysteries by the priestly sages, and for them this meant a kind of retirement from the outer world; they realized that if they were to reach what was to be attained they must lead a different life than they had so far lived openly, and above all that they must accustom themselves to another way of thinking. These Mysteries existed all over the world, among the Greeks and Romans and other peoples, as may be confirmed by referring to extensive literature which already exists. The pupils admitted to the Mysteries were taught something comparable with what is now called science or knowledge, but they did not receive it in the same way, for by what they experienced they became quite other beings. To them came the conviction that in every man there lives, deeply hidden and slumbering so that the ordinary consciousness knows it not, a higher man. Just as the ordinary man experiences the world through his senses and uses his thinking to reflect upon such experiences, so can this other man — at first unknown to external consciousness, but capable of being awakened in the depths of his nature — recognize another world unattainable by external sight and thought. This was called 'The birth of the inner man'. The expression is still used, though in these days it is dry and abstract in character and regarded lightly, but when the disciple of the Mysteries applied it to himself it stood for a tremendous event to be compared in some measure with being born in the physical sense. As man in the physical world is born out of a dark substratum (be it one of nature according to the materialistic idea, of a spiritual substratum in the view of spiritual science) so, physically speaking, there was really born through the processes of the Mysteries a higher man who previously had been as little present as was the human being before birth or conception. The disciple was a new-born being. The present view of knowledge, as given everywhere in answer to a deeply philo-sophic question, is exactly the opposite of that which formed the central point of the whole idea and outlook of the Mysteries. Today we ask, in the sense of Kant and Schopenhauer, 'Where lie the limits of knowledge? What is it in the power of man to know?'. We need only take up a newspaper to meet the answer that here or there lie the limits and that beyond them it is impossible to go. Certainly it was admitted in the Mysteries that there were problems which man could not solve, but it would never have been held in the sense of Kant or in Schopenhauer's *Theory of Cognition* that 'Man cannot know' this or that! What would have been appealed to was man's capability of development, to the powers lying dormant within him which must be evoked so that he might rise to higher capacities of knowledge. The question in those times resolved itself into what was to be done in order to get beyond that which in normal life is the boundary of knowledge; how to develop deeper powers in human nature.

Something more is needed if we are to feel the whole magic

charm of the Mysteries that, like a breath, pervades the works of
the exoteric writers, Plato, Aristides, Plutarch and Cicero. Here
we must be clear that the kind of mental comprehension present
in the forming of the disciples of the Mysteries was quite different
from that of the men of today when they confront scientific truths.
What we now call science is open to anybody and everybody in
any condition of receptivity whatever. It is just here that we
recognize the characteristic of truth, that it is independent of mood
and feeling. For the pupil of the Mysteries the most necessary thing
was that, before he was brought to the great truths, he should go
through something whereby his soul was transformed in his feelings and impressions. What today appears as a simple scientific
truth would not have been put to him so that he could grasp it
externally with his understanding, but his natural temperament
would have been prepared beforehand so that he could draw near
with reverential awe to what could approach him. Consequently
his preparation was not one of learning; it was a gradual and radical
transformation and education of his soul. The question was how
the soul approached the great truths and wisdom and how it reacted
to them, and hence arose the conviction that through the Mysteries
man was bound up and united with the very foundations of the
cosmos and with what flowed from the springs of all cosmic
beginnings.

Thus was the disciple prepared for the experiencing of something which is described by Aristides. Anyone who has lived
through what these disciples experienced as described in my
Knowledge of Higher Worlds and its Attainment can confirm this
himself. He knows that the words of Aristides correspond with
the truth when he writes, 'I seemed to be approaching God, I
seemed to feel His presence, and I was in a state between waking
and sleeping; my spirit was quite light — so light that no one who
was uninitiated could describe or understand it.' There was a way,
therefore, to the divine foundations of the universe which was
neither science nor one-sided religion, but consisted in a thorough
preparation of the soul, enabling it to sense the thoughts of the
gods permeating the evolution of the universe so that it might draw

near to God and those spiritual foundations. As we take in the external air with our breath and make it a part of our body, so did the disciple of the Mysteries receive into his soul that which pulsates spiritually through the universe until he was united with it and so became a new man permeated by the divinity.

Now, however, Anthroposophy or spiritual science shows that what was then possible was only an historical phenomenon in human evolution, and when the question arises as to whether the ancient Mysteries of pre-Christian times are still possible in the same way, it can only be said that historical research verily proves that what has just been described did really exist but that it exists no longer in the same form. The pre-Christian method of Initiation is now not possible. A man must indeed be short-sighted if he believes that the human soul is the same in all epochs, or that the spiritual path of the olden times holds good for the present. The path to the divine and primal sources of the world has now become another, and intellectual historical research shows that it did so in its very essence at the time ascribed by tradition to the events of Palestine. These events made a deep incision in the evolution of man. Something entered into human nature in the post-Christian period which entirely differed from what was there before. Such a method of thinking as is possible nowadays — the method of drawing nearer to the universe through scientific thought — did not exist in pre-Christian ages. The Mysteries did not conduct man in the manner described to the very highest treasures of wisdom in order that he might do something in secret, or acquire something special for himself as a member of a small circle, but because our modern way of combining thoughts through logic was not possible at that time. A glance at the history of humanity will show that in the course of two centuries, during the time of the Greek philosophers, the present mode of thinking was gradually prepared, and that only now has it reached the point of embracing external nature so wonderfully. Thus the entire form our consciousness takes and the way we create our conceptions of the universe differ entirely from pre-Christian times. For the moment we are only concerned with this fact as showing that human nature

has changed. A careful review of human evolution makes it clear
that consciousness has altered in the course of evolution (the
results arising from research are to be found in my *Occult Science*).
The men of old did not regard things and think about them as we
do with our senses and understanding; they had a kind of clairvoyance, but this was of a dim and dreamlike nature. Herein lies
the import of evolution, that an old clairvoyance which in primitive
times was spread over all humanity gave way to that form of
thought which we possess today. The ordinary inhabitants of every
country had this kind of clairvoyant power, and a path leading
from that to higher stages was provided in the Mysteries. Thereby
development was given to the normal soul-faculties of man.

Observation of the world by what we call reasoning and logic
having displaced the old clairvoyance, the latter is no longer a
natural faculty, but it lasted right through the historical period and
reached its culmination in the Graeco-Roman era during which
the appearance of Christ occurred. At that point of time collective
humanity everywhere had come so far in its evolution that the old
clairvoyance had passed away and the old Mysteries were no
longer possible. What then took the place of the old Mysteries
and what did man acquire through the Mysteries?

These were of two kinds: the one proceeded from that centre
of civilization which was afterwards occupied by the ancient
Persians, and the other was to be met with in its purest form in
Egypt and Greece. They were entirely different throughout those
times. It was the endeavour of all the Mysteries to produce in man
an extension of his soul-powers, but this was achieved in a different way in Greece and Egypt, than in Persia. In the two former,
which agreed essentially, the object was to effect in the disciples
a transformation of their soul-powers. This transformation took
place under a certain supposition which must be understood before
anything else. It was that in the depths of the soul there slumbers
another, a divine man; this hidden man originated from the same
sources from which the rock forms into crystal and the plant breaks
forth in the spring. Plants, however, had already utilized all that
was contained within them, whereas man, in so far as he had

understood himself and worked with his own powers, had remained an imperfect being, and that which was within him had only come to the fore after much endeavour. Appeal, therefore, in the Egyptian and Greek Mysteries was made to a spiritual, a divine inner man, and, when this was referred to, allusion was made also to the powers within the Earth. For according to the views held, the Earth was not regarded as the lifeless cosmic body of modern astronomy, but as a spiritual planetary being. In Egypt, when one wished to contemplate the origin and source of what could be experienced as manifestation of the inner man, reference was made to the wonderful spirit-forces and nature-force called by the names of Isis and Osiris. In Greece this primal source was referred to under the name of Dionysos. As a consequence of this, profane writers asserted that the nature and being of things were the objects sought for, and in the Greek Mysteries they called what was found of the forces of human nature the 'sub-earthly' portion of man, not the 'super-earthly'. The nature of the great 'daemons' was spoken of, and under this title was represented all that worked on the Earth of the nature of spiritual forces. The nature of these daemons (in a good sense) was sought for through that which man was to bring forth from himself. Then the disciple had to go through all the feelings and perceptions that were possible for him in the course of evolution. He had to experience what was meant by 'going down into the depths of his soul'; to learn that a fundamental feeling so dominated all soul-being that in ordinary life no conception of it could be formed, and that that feeling was a deep egoism — the almost unconquerable selfishness lying within the inner recesses of a human being. By means of struggling against and conquering all selfishness and egoism the disciple had to go through something for which we have today only an abstract expression, i.e. the feeling of all-inclusive love and compassion for men and beings. Compassion, in so far as the human soul was capable of it, was to take the place of selfishness. It was clearly understood that if the disciple evoked this compassion, which belonged in the first place to the hidden forces of the world of feeling, it could draw out from the depths of his soul the divine powers slumbering therein. It was held moreover that as he looked out upon the world with his ordinary understanding he must soon become aware of his powerlessness as a man with reference to the cosmos, and that the further he projected his conceptions and ideas the stronger this feeling grew until in the end he was led to doubt what indeed could be called knowledge, i.e. gnosis. Arrived at that point, he must then overcome this feeling of emptiness in his soul whenever he desired to encompass the cosmos with his ideas. This consciousness of a void was accompanied by fear and anxiety, and consequently the Greek disciple of Mysticism first filled himself with a dread of the unknown and then, by coupling this with compassion, drew forth the divine powers lying within him. So did he learn to transform fear into awe and reverence, and to realize how the highest kind of awe and reverential devotion for all the phenomena of the universe was able to penetrate every substance and conception that lay beyond the scope of ordinary knowledge.

Thus the Greek Mysteries, as also those of Isis and Osiris in the Egyptian Mysteries, worked outwards from the inmost nature of man and sought to lead him into the spiritual worlds. It was a living apprehension of the 'God in Man'. A real acquaintance was formed between man and God, and immortality ranked not as mere abstract theory and philosophy but as something known, something as firmly grounded as the knowledge of external colours, and this was experienced as an intimate connection with external things. With no less certainty was this experienced also in the Persian or Mithraic Mysteries. Whereas man was led in the Greek and Egyptian Mysteries through the unfettering of his soul-powers, he was confronted at once with the universe itself in the Mithraic Mysteries; not only did the universe work upon him through the great and mighty nature which is overlooked by those who regard the world in its external aspect, but by gaining a deep intimacy with nature he could gaze upon phenomena that lay outside the limits of the human understanding. By the methods then used, the most terrible and magnificent powers were brought before the pupil from universal space. Whereas the Greek disciple was affected by a deep feeling of reverence, to the Mithraic disciple alone was given the knowledge of the terrible and awe-inspiring powers in nature so that he felt himself infinitesimally small in comparison. So powerful was this impression, consequent upon his alienation from the primal source of being, that he felt that in its vastness the universe could at any moment overwhelm and annihilate him. The first impulse that came from his being led through a comprehensive astronomy and science away from external things to the greatness of the phenomena of the universe, and what he further developed in the Mysteries was then more a consequence of the truth in all its ramifications when nature in her details (science in the old sense of the word) worked upon his soul. The Greek disciple became fearless through the setting free of his powers. The Mithraic disciple was brought so far that he drank in the greatness of cosmic thought, and thereby his soul also became strong and courageous. A knowledge of the dignity and value of a human being was gained, and with it a feeling for truth and fidelity; the disciple learned to recognize that man must always hold himself under control during his earthly existence.

Such were the benefits obtained especially through the Mithraic Mysteries, and whereas the Greek and Egyptian Mysteries are to be found spread over Greece and Egypt, the Mithraic are diffused from Persia as far as the Caspian Sea, along the Danube into Germany, and even to the South of France, to Spain and to England. Europe was indeed permeated by the Mithraic Mysteries, and everywhere it was seen clearly that something streamed into man from the universe if only he could learn to understand it, and this that could be received was Mithra, the god that streams through the world in all worlds. It was through this power of action that courage was aroused: the warriors, the Roman legionaries, were filled with the Mithraic service or cult of Mithra. Both leaders and men were initiated into the Mysteries. Thus was God sought on the one hand by the freeing of the individual soul-powers, and it was quite evident that through this process something streamed out from the depths of the soul. On the other hand, however, it was equally evident that when

man sought God by devoting himself to the great cosmic phenomena, something streamed into his soul as the essence,
the finest life-sap contained in the world. There were found the
primordial forces of the universe. God came as it were into
human souls through this development which was attained in
the Mystery schools. A veritable process is to be seen here: each
soul became a door for the entrance of the godhead into human
evolution on earth. Few were able to undergo such a development,
and a special preparation for it was necessary. The teaching
consisted in showing that what was hidden in external nature
(Mithra), as also in the inner man of the Greek, poured through
the world as a stream of divine consecration.

The evolution of man has now changed, and the entire method
of Initiation is different. Here we touch upon what must be called
the Mystical Fact of the Christ Event. To penetrate deeply into
history is to see that the early Christians were more or less dimly
conscious that the same force which entered the soul only through
devotion to the Mysteries, to the divine principle of the universe
(streaming forth from cosmos as Mithra or out of the depths of the
soul as Dionysos), was as the deed of a unique cosmic divinity in
one single fact in the evolution of the Earth. That which was sought
for beyond this, and was not to be found except by those who
alienated themselves from outer life in the Mysteries, was at a given
time incorporated into the Earth by the divinity. No human effort
was needed, for the divinity once and for all permeated the being
of the Earth, and henceforth even those who had lost the power
to penetrate to the divine principle of the cosmos could meet Him
in another way. The god who could now penetrate into the human
soul (neither as Mithra from without nor Dionysos from within)
was Himself a fusion of Mithra and Dionysos, and also was related
to human nature in its depths. He was embraced and encompassed
by the name of CHRIST. Mithra and Dionysos were united in the
being who entered humanity in the Event of Palestine, and Christianity was the confluence of both cults. The Hebrews, who were
chosen that they might provide the necessary body through which
this Event might take place, had become acquainted with the Mithraic

and Dionysian cults, but they remained far removed from either. The Greek thought of himself as a weak man who must develop deeper powers before he could penetrate into the depths of his soul, while the follower of Mithra felt that by letting the whole surrounding sphere of the air work upon him he might become united with the divine qualities of the universe. The Hebrew, on the other hand, held that the deeper human nature, with all that was hidden within it, was already there in the first Man, and the ancient Hebrews called this primal man Adam. According to old Hebraic ideas, that which man could seek, and which joined him with the divine, was present originally in Adam, but in course of evolution the descendants of each generation became further and further removed from the source of existence. Being 'subject to original sin', as they put it, meant that man had not remained as he was and had been ejected from the sphere of the divine; regarding himself as standing below Adam he sought the reason in original sin. But though less than that which lived in the depths of human nature, he could unite himself with the deeper powers and thereby be raised again. This point of view, that once man had stood higher and that through the qualities connected with the blood ties he had lost something, was an historical one. What the adherent of the Mithraic Mysteries saw in humanity as one whole the Hebrew saw in his own nation and was conscious that its original source had been lost. So that while among the Persians there was a kind of training of the consciousness, there was among the ancient Hebrews a consciousness of a historical development: Adam, by falling into sin, had fallen from the heights where he once stood. Consequently the Hebrews were the best prepared for the thought that that which had happened at the initial point of evolution (and which had brought about a deterioration in humanity) could only be raised again through an historical Event, i.e. by something actually taking place in the spiritual substrata of the Earth's being. The ancient Hebrew who rightly understood evolution felt that the Mithra god, equally with the god who is evoked from the depths of the human soul, could come down without man going through a development in the Mysteries.

Thus in these people, and above all in the case of John the

Baptist, there arose a consciousness of the fact that what the
Mysteries had handed down in the form of Dionysos and Mithra
was born at one and the same time in one Man. Those of them
who felt this in a deeper sense held that even as through Adam
the descent of man into the world was brought about (all men
having descended from one forefather and inherited from him all
the deeper forces that lead to sin and error) so, through one being
who descends from the spiritual worlds as the union of Mithra
and Dionysos, must the initial point be formed to which men can
look when they have to rise again. As in the Mysteries human
nature was developed through the setting free of the deeper soul
forces or through a view of the cosmos, the Hebrews now saw
in the god who came down into physical being Him on whom the
soul must look and believe, for whom it must develop the deepest
love, and who as the great example could lead them back to their
divine origin.

He who had the profoundest knowledge of this fact of Christianity was Paul. The Apostle recognized that as men looked to
Adam as their physical progenitor they could, through the Christ
Impulse, look to the Christ as the great example, and so attain to
what was striven for in the Mysteries and must be born again if
they were to know their own original nature. The knowledge that
was kept within the recesses of the temples, and could only be
attained after ascetic training, was set forth neither in mundane
documents nor as some external fact but as having been accomplished as a mystical fact, the god who pervaded the world having
actually appeared in one single form. What the disciples of the
Mithraic Mysteries acquired through looking upon the greatest
model had now been attained through Christ. The courage, self
control and energy acquired by those disciples had also to be
acquired by those who could no longer be initiated in the old
Mithraic sense; through the model of the historical Christ and the
gazing upon Him the impulse towards this fortitude was now to
pour itself out upon the soul. In the Mithraic Mysteries, as has
been shown, the whole universe was in a certain sense born in
the soul of the disciple, and the courageous soul was fired with

all the inner forces of initiative. In the baptism of John something was poured down from above of which human nature could be the vehicle; when man was permeated with the thought that his nature was capable of assimilating the profoundest harmony of the universe, the view of the baptism aroused within him the understanding that Mithra could be born in human nature. Those, therefore, who grasped the original meaning of Christianity, acknowledged that the end of the Mysteries had come: the god who formerly had poured Himself into the Mysteries had now flowed directly into the being of the Earth through the personality who stood at the beginning of a new era (our present one).

The connection with the Greek or Dionysian Mysteries has now to be considered. Through the fact that the human gaze was guided to Jesus of Nazareth in whom Mithra lived and who then passed through death, an indication was given that Mithra (the bestower of courage, self control and energy) had himself died with the death of Jesus. It was further seen that, because Mithra had so vanished, that which man found in his deepest nature, and had attained earlier through the Dionysian Mysteries, had now become in Jesus of Nazareth the immortal conqueror over death. Herein lies the true Christian meaning of the Resurrection if it is grasped in its spiritually scientific sense. The baptism by John in the Jordan demonstrated that the old Mithra had entered into man, that thereby human nature had won the victory over death, and that by the example so created the soul could unite itself in the deepest love in order to come to that which lived in its own depths. In the Risen Christ was seen the fact that man, by living according to the Event that had taken place in history, could rise above the level of ordinary humanity.

Thus in the centre of the history of the world was set an historical event in the place of that which had been sought in the Mysteries times without number. The great revelation that came to St. Paul was that human nature had thereby become different, and this was concealed within what is known as 'The Event of Damascus'. Writing of what he experienced before Damascus, the Apostle relates how he learned to understand, not from external documents but through a purely spiritual clairvoyant experience, that the moment when the Incarnation itself should take place in an historical personage had already passed. The existence of Christ as a real man could never be experienced by Paul through an external fact, and what he could learn in Palestine did not convince him that the union of Mithra and Dionysos had lived in Jesus of Nazareth. But when, before Damascus, his spiritual sight was opened, it became clear that a god who could be called by the name of Christ not only worked through the world as a supersensible being but had actually come to Earth and conquered death. Henceforth he preached that what for the Initiates had previously been a streaming substance was now to be found as continuous historical fact. This lies at the basis of his words, 'If Christ be not risen then is our preaching vain, and your faith is also vain.'

Such was the path by which Paul came to Jesus by the indirect way of Christ, it being clear to him that something had taken place in Palestine which previously could only be experienced in the Mysteries. And this still applies today. Because Christ is the focus of all human development and the highest example for the inmost powers of the soul the bond established with Him must be of the most intimate kind. To become a disciple it is required of a man that he set little value upon his own life, and so it must be regarded as of small importance to lay aside all documentary evidence and historical traditions in order to come to Christ. Indeed there is cause for thankfulness that the fact that there ever was an historical Christ Jesus cannot be established, for no document could prove that He was the most significant of all that has passed into humanity.

The connection between Christ and the ancient Mysteries is therefore quite clear. The disciples of the latter had to go through what may be called intimate soul experiences in order to come to God; their inner feelings and sensations were more lively and intense than those of the ordinary man, and so they became aware that they were set fast in a lower nature which hindered them from arriving at the sources of being. This lower nature was indeed a seducer leading them away from the upward path, and that which so allured them had also become their own lower nature, and herein lay the 'Temptation' that came to every disciple of the Mysteries. At the moment when God awoke within them they became aware also of their lower or sensual natures. It was as though some strange unknown being were urging them not to follow the unsubstantial and airy heights of the spiritual world, but to seize the coarse and material things that lay close at hand. Each disciple had to pass through a time when everything spiritual seemed unreal in comparison with the ordinary way of looking at things, and all that was connected with the senses appeared alluring as against the stress of spiritual effort. At another stage in mystic development these lower forces were overcome, a higher outlook being attained with the growth of invigorated powers of courage and so forth. All this teaching was clothed in certain instructions that may be verified from the writings of exoteric authors, as also in the methods of Initiation given by spiritual science and set forth in *Occult Science*. There were various methods both in the Greek and the Mithraic Mysteries. Finally the disciples experienced the 'at-one-ment' with Him who was the divine Man, but here the methods were different and varied widely in the many countries where Initiation existed.

In my *Christianity as Mystical Fact* the purpose is to show that in the Gospels nothing is to be met with but a rebirth of old Initiation instructions. What took place externally had already taken place similarly in the course of the Mysteries, and therefore the divine being who was in Jesus of Nazareth after the descent of the Mithra being had to experience the 'Temptation'. As the Tempter came on a small scale to the pupil of the Mysteries so did he also confront the God become Man. All that was true in the Mysteries is to be found repeated in the Gospel records which were new versions of the old inscriptions and instructions given in the Initiations. The writers of the Gospels saw that once that which hitherto had lain only in the Mysteries had been enacted on the plane of cosmic history, it was permissible to describe it in the same words as those in which their directions for Initiation were recorded. It is for this very reason that the Gospels were not intended to be biographies of Him who was the vehicle for the Christ. This is just the mistake of all modern criticisms of the Gospels. At the time they were written the sole object was to lead the human soul to a real love for the Great Soul, the source of the world's existence. Strangely enough a clear consciousness of this prevailed almost to the end of the eighteenth century. It is pointed out in isolated writings of remarkable interest that through the Gospels the soul can be so transformed as to find the Christ. Old Meister Eckhardt writes, 'Some people want to look at God with their eyes as they look at a cow, and want to love God as they love a cow. They love God as an outward possession and an inward comfort, but these people do not love Him aright. ... Simple folk imagine they ought to see God as if He stood there and they here; it is not so; God and I are one in recognition.' In another passage he writes, 'A Master says, "God has become man, and thereby the whole human race is raised in dignity. We may rejoice that Christ our brother has through His own power passed beyond the choir of angels, and sits at the right hand of the Father". This Master has spoken rightly, but verily I do not pay much attention to it. What help would it be to me if I had a brother who was a rich man, and I was at the same time a poor one? How would it help me if I had a brother who was a wise man, and I myself a fool? ... The heavenly Father begat His only Son in Himself and in me. Why in Himself and in me? I am one with Him, and it is not possible for Him to exclude me. In the same work the Holy Ghost received his being, and is from me as from God. Why? I am in God, and if the Holy Ghost does not receive his being from me neither does he receive it from God. I am in no way excluded.'

That is the point: that man through mystic development, without external mysteries but through the simple evolution of the soul, will in later times be able to experience that which was once experienced in the Mysteries. This, however, will only be possible because the Christ Event took place. Even if there were no Gospels, no records and no traditions, he who experiences the Christ in himself along with the being filled with Christ has the certainty, as St. Paul had it, that at the beginning of our era Christ was incarnated in a physical body. An historical biography of Jesus of Nazareth can never be gathered out of the Gospels, but through the right unfolding of his soul powers man can and must raise himself up to the Christ, and through the Christ to Jesus. Thus only can be understood what was the aim of the Gospels and what was lacking in the whole of the nineteenth century researches on the subject of Jesus. The picture of the Christ was allowed to recede into the background in order to present a tangible Jesus quite externally from the historical records. The Gospels were misunderstood, and consequently the methods of investigation crumbled to pieces.

Herewith the way is at the same time made clear to spiritual science. Its object is to show what are the deeper powers that have lain in man since the coming of Christ, and which he can develop. Not in the depths of externally appointed Mysteries, but in the stillness of his room, man can attain, by devoting himself to what happened in Palestine, that which was attained by the disciples of the Mysteries. By experiencing the Christ within himself he gains in courage and energy and in a consciousness of his dignity as man, and comes to the knowledge of how he has to take his place in humanity in the right sense. And at the same time he experiences, as could the adherent of the Greek Mysteries, the universal love which lives in Christ and embraces all external creatures. He learns never to be afraid or to despair in the face of the world, and freely and humbly devotes himself to the secrets of the universe.

All this comes to the man who permeates himself with the Mystical Fact of Christianity, the successor of the old Mysteries. Simply through a cognitional development of these fundamental thoughts the Historical Jesus becomes a fact for those who have a deep knowledge of Christ. In Western philosophy it was said that without eyes none could see colour nor hear without ears; the universe would be without light and sound. True as this is with regard to seeing and hearing, it is equally true that without light no eye could have come into existence nor could man have had any perceptions connected with it. As Goethe says, 'If the eye were not born of like nature to the sun it could never look upon the sun', and 'The eye is a creation of the light'.

The mystical Christ, spoken of by those whose spiritual sight is opened and who behold Him as Paul did, was not always in man. In pre-Christian times He was unattainable in any development through the Mysteries in the way in which He was to be found after the Mystery of Golgotha. That there might be an inner Christ and that the higher man could be born, an historical Christ was needed, the Incarnation of the Christ in Jesus. As the eye can originate only through the effect of light, so, in order that there could be a mystical Christ, the historical Christ must have been there. Had there been no documents containing a biography of Jesus of Nazareth this could still be said and felt, for Jesus is not to be recognized through external writings. This fact was long known in the evolution of the West and will again be known. Spiritual science will so formulate it that it can draw together from out of its various spheres what will lead to a real understanding of the Christ, and thereby to an understanding of Jesus. It has come about that Jesus has been actually alienated from the world and the methods of the Jesus investigations have melted away, but the deepening of ourselves in the Christ being (in the Christ as a being) will lead to a recognition of the greatness of Jesus of Nazareth.

This path, by which the Christ is first recognized through inward soul experience, leads through what really has developed out of the soul to the understanding of the Mystical Fact of Christianity, and of the gradual development of humanity, as being such that the Christ Event must take place within it as the most significant point in the evolution of man. The way leads through the Christ to Jesus. The Christ Idea bears fruitful seed that will bring humanity not merely to the apprehension of a general pantheistic cosmic spirit, but the individual man to the understanding of his own history; as he feels his Earth to be bound up with all cosmic existence so will he recognize that his past is bound up with a supersensible and super-historical Event. This Event is that the Christ being stands as a supersensible Mystical Fact at the middle of human evolution. He will be recognized as such by the humanity of the future apart from all external historical research and documents. Christ will remain the strong cornerstone of mankind's evolution. Man will bring the forces out of himself to renew his own history, and therewith also the history of the evolution of the world.